The Church of God

FOUNDATIONS FOR FAITH

General editor: Peter Toon

Other titles in the series

FOUNDATIONS FOR FAITH

The Church of God

George M. Newlands

Marshall Morgan & Scott

For Stewart, Murray and Craig

Marshall Morgan & Scott
3 Beggarwood Lane, Basingstoke, Hants, UK
Copyright © George Newlands 1984
First published by Marshall Morgan & Scott 1984

ISBN: 0 551 01019 3

Photoset, printed and bound in Great Britain by
Redwood Burn Limited, Trowbridge, Wiltshire

Contents

Preface

The purpose of this book is to provide a compact but still reasonably comprehensive account of the nature and activity of the Christian Church. The book looks at the development of Church, ministry and sacraments up to the present day, and beyond this to consider requirements for the effective ministry of the Church in the future.

I concentrate on the central questions and provide a reliable guide to the main features of doctrinal development. In addition I attempt to express my own theological understanding of the Church, indicating how this arises, what sort of selections are made from the manifold assortment of data, and for what reasons. I have written for college students and other readers committed to or at least open to exploration of the central concerns of the Christian Church. My own views, clearly, are not infallible, and are expressed to provoke rather than to inhibit critical reflection.

As a Scots Presbyterian minister teaching in the Cambridge Divinity Faculty, where my friends, colleagues and students are mainly Anglican, but also Catholic, Methodist and other besides, I hope that I may be able, sometimes at least, to consider the Church from more than a narrowly sectarian point of view. The most successful ecumenical communication is not always consciously 'ecumenical'. This can lead to theological obscurity, and even a 'consensus' of churchmen may be then quite unintelligible to the world which the Church of Jesus Christ is called to serve. However, it may be taken that I have considerable sympathy with H. R. Niebuhr's comment, in his fine study *The Social Sources of Denominationalism*, that 'Denominational Christianity offers no hope to the divided world. From it the world can expect none of the prophetic guidance it requires ... The road to unity is the road of repentance.' Without the usual generous help with bibliography and ideas from the many traditions locally represented this study would scarcely have got off the ground. I am grateful to the publishers and to the Revd Dr Peter Toon, the editor of this series, for their kind invitation to write this book.

My thanks also to two of the authors in this series, my colleague the Revd Brian L. Hebblethwaite, Dean of Chapel at Queens' College, Cambridge, and my father-in-law, the Revd Professor Ronald S. Wallace, for a number of most valuable comments on the manuscript. I am much indebted to my wife who made it possible for me to have the time to write, to my small sons who saw rather less than usual of their father last summer vacation, and once again, to Hazel and Gerald Hedge for the final typescript.

Cambridge, Advent, 1979

PART I

FOUNDATIONS

1 What is the Christian Church?

THINKING ABOUT THE CHURCH

Somewhere in your neighbourhood there is probably a building which is called a church, unless you live in a part of the world where churches are banned. It may be a dilapidated corrugated iron hut. It may be a facade that has seen better days, a splendid neo-Gothic edifice like the tower of St John's College Chapel which I see from my window as I write these lines; it may be a daring piece of modern architecture. It may remind you of affluence or complacency, of poverty or resentment, of the peace of God, the folly of men, or any sort of combination of these images or others. You will very probably link it with other ideas, associated with the town or village in which you live. It may be thought of in connection with your family life, the place in which you were brought up, the political and economic structures of the society in which you live, for better or for worse. You may prefer to see the church as something separate from all these things, also for better or for worse. You may think of it as the symbol of a question mark to set, occasionally at least, against its environment, against itself, and against your own reflections.

Thinking about the Church may make you excited or apathetic, may invite to laughter or tears. If you can read these words, and have at least the option of entering a church, then you are one of the lucky ones. After all, most of the world's human population to date has lived and died unable to read, to write, to be aware of a caring community of the sort that we tend to take for granted.[1] Even in comparatively recent times work has often been too all-embracing, nations too socially divided, to enable the whole population to have the option of full participation in the Church.

Today, at least in many parts of the world, the opportunities for participation are much greater. Yet the Church appears often to be in decline, at least in the West. If this were all that is to be said, then that may be unfortunate, but there may be nothing to be done. Institutions come and go with civilisations and cultures. Just as it would be tedious, not to say disastrous, if people never died, if gardens never faded in autumn, so with all our institutions.

The Church claims to be more than another multi-national institution, another weekend leisure activity. The Christian Church claims to be the Church of God, the gathering of the people of God for the service of all humanity in the name of Jesus Christ. It may of course be argued that there have always been religions with absolute claims. Thousands of ancient deities have come and gone, with their accompanying devotees and shrines. To be a god is by definition to claim absolute status, freedom from change and decay. The fate of the gods is not exposure but obsolescence. They are not disproved, but are quietly deposited in the better sort of national museum, visited by tourists and commemorated in academic dissertations.

Such a fate, it may be argued, has already befallen the God of the Christians and his Church. Evidence can be marshalled for this conclusion, and if sufficient evidence is forthcoming, there is no more to be said. Part of the purpose of this book is to indicate grounds for thinking that, sometimes almost despite all appearances, the Christian Church is still and always will be central to the well-being of mankind.

THE CHURCH AND THE LOVE OF GOD

Conceptions of what the Church is and ought to be differ enormously among various Christian groups, not to speak of views held by people with no personal affinity to Christian faith. Different denominations have different views. Within and across denominations there are deeply significant differences of perspective. Fundamentalist communities of various colours, whether biblical, cultural or political fundamentalists, have very precise and definite understandings of Church.[2] Consciously liberal Christians have other perspectives, and there are all sorts of unlikely combinations of more or less liberal views. There is too a significant section of the community which has no formal Church membership but is nevertheless attracted to the Christian gospel and basically sympathetic to Christian values, moral and religious.

It would be optimistic to expect, within the confines of a short volume, to fulfil the expectations and echo the commitments of all such groups. Apart from content each has its own expectations, more or less formally articulated, of what theological method should be, of how the questions can be best approached. I hope to try throughout to remain aware of some of these contrasting expectations and sensitivities, so that it becomes possible to present a study of the doctrine of the Church, past and present, in which most people who place serious value on the Christian gospel may find at least something worthy of further attention and reflection.

The importance of the Church is entirely dependent on the truth of the Christian gospel. If the gospel were to be shown to be mistaken, then it might be thought that the Church could still fulfil a vital role in providing charitable work and fostering social cohesion. But then its character and central purpose would have changed decisively. The truth of the gospel and its message about the nature of God and his purpose for humanity is in no way dependent on the activities of the Church. God is not God because we say so. Justification of belief in the Christian God provides no automatic justification for belief in the Church in any of its institutional forms. Yet the two issues of the intellectual and the social credibility of the Church as God's Church, though clearly distinguished, are still related. If we believe in the Christian God, we are bound to be concerned with his purposes for mankind and so with Christian community in its various forms and our own participation in this.

Basically then the Church is about God, about the life of the creator of the universe in relation to his creation. The meaning of the gospel message of the love of God for mankind expressed through Jesus Christ cannot be reduced to one authorised definition, and its realisation in human life takes various forms. I find it easiest to express my own understanding of God in this way: The Christian God is in his essential nature love. This love is expressed precisely in the self-giving, self-affirming involvement of God in the life, death and resurrection of Jesus of Nazareth, and in God's present relationship to all humanity through the Spirit of the risen Christ. In the New Testament God is identified with his creatures through his presence in Jesus, suffering, sharing in life and death, sharing Jesus' lot, somehow even taking death overcome into his own future activity as God. To say this is not of course to explain, far less resolve, the mystery of God's being, which remains in many respects mysterious to us in faith. God is revealed in Christ precisely as the hidden God. It is to indicate wherein the mystery lies, in God's distinctive character as overwhelming love.[3]

MINISTERS OF THE LOVE OF GOD

We may now set the scene for further study by taking a look at some familiar landmarks in thinking about Christian community. Christians have traditionally understood themselves through the use of many powerful images. One of these is that of the people of God. This has sometimes been understood in an exclusive sense but it need not be so. Of course the various peoples of the Old Testament, as well as of the New Testament, came to understand themselves as the people of God. Followers of other religions also understand themselves as the people of God. Non-religious people rightly resent their relegation by definition to the role of inferior beings. For Christianity all mankind is the people for whom God has involved himself in death and to whom he has brought new life. That part of humanity which constitutes the Christian Church consists of the people who are committed to the gospel implications of the service of Jesus Christ for all mankind.

To be committed to the service of Jesus Christ for all mankind is to be a minister of the Christian gospel. All Christians are ministers in this basic sense. There are other, more specialised forms of ministry. This brings us to the long tradition of a doctrine of the ministry. Ministry and priesthood, like church, parliament and pop-corn, are all terms with colourful cultural connotations. Ministry may suggest prelates or pension funds, hopeless amateurism or slippery professionalism, selfless service or servitude. Institutions need both professional structures and professional servants if they are not to be inefficient, and if they are to be preserved from all the vagaries of romantic individualism and collective inertia. Beyond this the Christian ministry in all its branches has always been understood to be devoted to discipleship, to the service of God, in order to serve God's purpose in the world. This is at once its charter and its humiliation. It is the ministry of the word of God that we shall want to think about further. This ministry may not perhaps be divorced entirely from questions about the appropriate structures of social engineering. But it goes beyond these questions. Here as at every point the dominical question 'What do ye more than others?' becomes directly and often embarrassingly relevant to Christian service.

The ministry of all Christians, as much as the ministry of those ordained to the traditional service of full time ministry, ought to be given over to the implementation of love for all mankind in the concrete working out of concern for the physical and mental well-being of our neighbours. Since ministry is above all the means by which we may become the instruments of God's love in the world, we who are Christians are bidden to be the messengers of God's word of salvation in proclaiming the gospel and helping people to become aware of God's presence to them as God. Here is the whole field of Christian communication, in preaching and in action.

GOD'S CHURCH

The field of Christian communication includes too the whole area of sacramental theology. Christians may understand Jesus Christ as God's sacrament for the world, and it is open to us to share in, and to invite others to share in this spiritual dimension. We shall want to explore carefully the dimensions of sacrament, spirituality and mystery. These are sometimes confused with magic, pietism and mystification. In this way a whole area of the gospel may be barred, to the impoverishment of many, often deeply thoughtful Christians. In thinking of spirituality we shall be concerned with the providential activity in Church and world of the God whom Christians have traditionally understood as Father, Son and Holy Spirit. The doctrine of the Holy Spirit embraces more than the sphere of the Church alone, and involves the whole manner of God's action in history.

It cannot be emphasised too much that in speaking of the Church we are thinking of a means to an end rather than an end in itself, of what Bonhoeffer called 'the penultimate things' rather than 'the last things'.[4] Christians understand the church to be called the instrument of God's love for the salvation of mankind through Christ. Like its Lord, it must lose its life to find it. This does not make the Church's activity in the present superfluous. On the contrary, those who await 'the last things' as the fulfilment of God's eschatological kingdom of love in the communion of saints have a particular incentive to live in society according to this eschatological purpose here and now. On this understanding the Church becomes not increasingly redundant but increasingly relevant to the human future as God's future.

Balance here is everything. We have to try to grasp the nettle of living according to the perspectives of the gospel. We have to avoid the easy option of disregarding public standards of rationality. We may not lapse into a private language of revelation, with all its attendant cosy irresponsibility. This is a perennial Christian challenge, to be faced in every generation.

The basic Christian reality is the reality of God, of his creative relationship with all mankind, and of his relationship with Christians through Jesus Christ in word and sacrament. To describe this reality as 'the Church' is too narrow, though this relationship is the centre of the Church's witness. Karl Barth was undoubtedly right in the 1920s in taking exception to Christian attempts to see the twentieth century as 'the century of the Church', humorously caricaturing such an idea as 'the century of the purple'. As he said in a speech against Nazism at a time of considerable personal danger, 'The gospel means, purely and simply, not men for God but God for men'.[5] Not the human organisation but the divine grace is prior, not the Church for its own sake but for the sake of God's love for mankind.

TOWARDS A DOCTRINE OF THE CHURCH

Having set the scene and established some priorities we must now come closer to the concrete task of working out a doctrine of the Church. The doctrine is best seen as an eschatological idea. For us it is given only to stand, if we can, on the shoulders of those who have come before us and hope to see the present a little more clearly. We may then be able to make some small contribution to the ongoing quest of faith seeking understanding.

As with all Christian doctrines, and indeed with intellectual formulation in most areas of human endeavour, there appear from the literature available to be almost as many doctrines of the Church as there are branches of the Church and theologians in it. We must look briefly at the biblical material, the historical development, contemporary theory, and then try to build on the basis of these foundations.

There tends to be a certain predictability in studies of the Church. Roman Catholics interpret the biblical evidence in one way, treat historical development in a corresponding manner, and then find their preferred doctrines of the Church, ministry and sacraments arising out of 'the facts'. Various sorts of Protestants do the same, arriving by a similar method at different results. More recently there has been a change. Catholics have used Protestant exegetical and historical methods and vice versa, while still contriving by a complex hermeneutical process to reach the 'expected' results, slightly modernised.[6] One cannot always predict that conservative scholars will reach uniformly conservative results and liberal scholars liberal results. For it appears that many who happily dismiss revelation and providence, incarnation and trinity, are prepared to die in the last ditch for historically indefensible doctrines of male episcopal apostolic succession of the most 'fundamentalist' sort, while others, passionate defenders of traditional Christology, have hardly any sense of Church, ministry and sacraments.

There are further intriguing complications. Though all Christians are clear that the Bible plays a basic role in theology, the uses of the Bible in theology are far from agreed among scholars. The biblical writers were themselves part of an ongoing tradition, oral and written, making selections and interpretations as they wrote, within the life and worship of the various early communities.

In the face of this diversity, some theologians have found refuge in the Fathers. For some confessions, their authority is decisive. The Fathers too interpreted scripture in their own ways, within the cultural and intellectual frame-works of the societies in which they worked, often borrowing exegetical techniques from non-biblical exegetes. Like their biblical predecessors, they too were working in a tradition, a tradition which, deepened and widened by a thousand years of further reflection, continued through the Reformation and beyond.

At the Reformation Luther's rediscovery of the Pauline gospel brought a much needed new emphasis on God's grace into the exegetical discussion. If Reformation brought a deeper theological perspective, the development of historico-critical exegesis in the eighteenth and nineteenth centuries appeared to bring a new objectivity into exegesis. At last we could use scientific method to determine 'what actually happened' in the biblical history. But despite the tangible progress, it became increasingly clear that when theologians use the Bible in theology, as in working out foundations for a doctrine of the Church, they are not approaching the subject with a clean slate, a blank, open mind, with the complete scholarly impartiality once imagined. The words are simply too hallowed by tradition, sacred, cultural and scholarly.

Such a discovery of the cultural relativity of our own interpretation need not however be an invitation to scepticism, complete cultural relativism or any sort of despondency. Even if we may have to be more modest in our claims to complete objectivity, we may be more sensitive in our awareness of the role of interpretation in the whole tradition of the gospel, and so may be able to come nearer the truth of the matter than before. At least, we may be able to hand on a better basis for further study.

We come now to the detail of the biblical narratives. These narratives may not furnish us with a complete doctrine of the Church. But they remain a central and absolutely indispensable element in the formulation of doctrine. In using the Bible we must make selections and form theological judgements, based on our understanding of the gospel as the story of God's love as it is spelled out in the biblical narratives as a whole. There is a constant dialogue between the particular text and the whole biblical context, and the life of the Christian community through the ages. To this dialogue the Bible remains central. For without this centre the gospel may become simply the reflection of our own private whims, and the Church the reflection of our cultural environment and no more, self-fulfilling in its prophecy and self-justifying in its action. This also happens to communities steeped in the Bible, and they are doubly without excuse. For it is, in a famous phrase of von Rad, in the double choir of those who come before and who come after that the gospel is to be understood, and it is in this context that the scriptures, in Luther's phrase, 'show forth Christ'.

2 The Church as the death of the gospel?

THE PRESENT SITUATION

This is a book about the Church. Can we really regard the Church as still having a claim to be considered as the servant of the gospel and the instrument of God's love in our time? It is important to pause and take stock of this question before proceeding happily further. However eminently reasonable theological treatises on the Church may sound, can we really regard the Church as any more than distantly related to the gospel of God in the life, death and resurrection of Jesus Christ? This is an issue which we need to stop and think about.

For people who are not Christians, the role of the Church in society may be seen as a record partly of shining humanitarian service, partly of disgraceful exploitation, partly of indifferent self-perpetuation. This record it shares with numerous other institutions. Even for Christians, for those who maintain faith in the God of love in spite of the manifold difficulties which arise, doubts about the Church invariably exist. Theological students of conservative as well as liberal opinion come in to find me writing these chapters and ask incredulously, 'Why on earth are you writing a book about the Church? Christology, God, man or salvation, yes; but the Church?'

The activities of the Church in the political catastrophes of the century have not always been edifying. Bonhoeffer said that 'Only those who speak up for the Jews have the right to sing hymns in church.' The Christian record against Nazism, of courageous witness by people in the widest spectrum from extreme liberalism to biblical pietism was deeply impressive. Anti-Semitism was not of course confined to Germany.[1] Too often the Church has been the death of the gospel. Through history it has supported totalitarian regimes to the right and the left. It has encouraged atrocity and benefited from exploitation. Dostoevsky's Grand Inquisitor is himself a formidable piece of evidence against belief in a God of love who permits innocent suffering and supports persecution through his representatives for the sake of some eschatological good purpose. We may say of course that the Church is bound to reflect the cultural standards of the time and must not be judged too harshly. The question of the gospel remains: What do ye *more* than others? More often perhaps the Church has acted in ignorance or partial ignorance of the real state of affairs. It is best not to know too much, better to compromise and prevent worse evil. A good example of the results of this attitude can be seen in the well-documented compulsory sterilisation of thousands of supposedly mentally unstable patients in the hospitals of the Inner Mission in Germany in 1934–5.[2] There were soon to be worse things going on, notably in the Far East, and there still are. But this is scarcely an excuse.

However inevitable wars may sometimes be, this half-guilty ignorance is a most serious problem for those who are called to take up the cross and follow Christ. In his outrageous but telling satire *Slaughterhouse Five*, Kurt Vonnegut makes this point precisely in speaking of the ignorance among a group of British prisoners of war of the origins of their soap and candles in the bodies of murdered Jews. Auschwitz or Dresden may be in danger of appearing to become almost commonplace in the light of continuing horrors. The Church has a duty to look at itself fairly carefully before marching confidently onward as before.

TENSION BETWEEN CHURCH AND GOSPEL

It is not necessary, however, to look at dramatic examples in order to feel the tension between the Church and the gospel. In the middle ages the Church was, at least in theory, in the centre of community life. Today it is the apparent global irrelevance of the Church which causes concern. Unless we are brought up in cathedral close or suburban Christian community we may find it hard to come in contact with the Church as an integral component of ordinary life. In the novel just mentioned, the sheer banality and triviality of the contacts which Billy Pilgrim and his mother have with the church indicates a state of affairs which fortunately is not universal but still exists.[3]

When I was a young assistant minister I used to compare notes with my wife and other colleagues who were working in similar parishes characterised by tall blocks of flats and low incomes. Reactions to the Church varied from place to place, from one side of a street to another if the parish boundary ran that way. In some parishes the church and the manse were the instinctive sources of immediate help in any circumstances at any time. The members of the church were regarded as an integral part of the community, as the basic resource, especially in the evenings when the social work professionals and others had gone home to their more up-market parts of the city. In other areas the church was felt to isolate itself from the rest of the community by an invisible but almost perceptible line. To become a member of the church was regarded, at least by the congregation, as having 'made it'. Those who had made it, socially and spiritually, were concerned more, it sometimes seemed, with the preservation of group identity than with identification with the rest of the community. If the members of the local church youth club broke windows, then the club should be closed. Let them go elsewhere, if they cannot respect church property.

It is easy to look back with amused disapproval on such a situation from the safety of the ivory tower. Where people have worked hard to build up a congregation, have sacrificed to produce buildings and amenities, it is not easy to be tolerant of those who seem to care little for the achievements or for the faith of the Church. If the Church is to gain credibility in society, so that men and women may be confronted with the scandal of the gospel rather than the scandal of the Church, it has no option but to lose its life in order to find it. This obviously does not mean neglecting congregational and community life and the material resources that make this possible. But if the Church is not to be the death of the gospel, then the service of Christ must clearly not be totally discontinuous with the imitation of Christ.

The gospel is not just about action. It is also about the understanding of God and the life of devotion to God through prayer and worship. If the Church is too much lost in pious contemplation, in closed fellowship, clearly it is unlikely to be able to speak to those who, outside the magic circle, are interested in the gospel but at the same time concerned to understand the Christian faith in relation to the rest of their lives. Closed communities do of course attract converts by their very exclusivity. Sudden conversions and reorientations take place. But if the gospel is invitation to fullness of life rather than command to unthinking obedience, of the sort practised throughout the world in numerous esoteric spiritual groups, then exclusivity is a luxury which the servants of Christ cannot afford.

Having said this, a church community which has no distinctively Christian character, which merely reflects the moral and intellectual values and conventions of the day, is clearly less than effectively witnessing to the gospel. Where such reflection of popular opinion is comparatively harmless the Church is just weak. Where society becomes oppressive the Church is an accomplice in oppression. Either way, the gospel is heard despite rather than because of the Church.

These examples are necessarily selective. I do not think it necessary to write at length on this theme. The Church has often been, humanly speaking, the death of the gospel. But it need not be, and often has not been. If the word were not preached through the Christian Church, the word would not be preached. If there were no example of caring for one another and for society within the Christian community, there would be no visible historical witness to God's love for mankind through Jesus Christ. We cannot have the gospel without the Church.

In a wider sphere of the Church in relation to society in its moral, political and social dimensions there are many areas in which the Church has made and can make a tangible difference, for good or for ill. To take one example, in many respects the Church appears to have copied rather than corrected ancient cultural usages which have assumed the dominance of the male and the subjection of the female in human society.[4] Here there is opportunity for the Church to give a lead in an enlightened direction. We shall return to the role of Church in society in detail in a separate chapter. Comparing the record of the Church with the gospel is inevitably a sobering process. Though the gospel is inevitably a judgement on the Church, it remains its unique source of strength and renewal.

THE CHURCH AND THE SPIRIT

It is one of the strange paradoxes of the Christian faith, not to be abused but of basic significance, that the power of God is made perfect in weakness. It is then perhaps appropriate that at the end of this section on the Church as the death of the gospel we should speak of the Church in the power of the Holy Spirit. Sometimes invocation of the Spirit in Church history has led to loss of touch with the harsh realities of life for most of the world's population, and to a proud and boastful self-confidence in the infallibility of ecclesiastical institutions, their opinions and their policies. This is not how St Paul understood the role of the Spirit. Without the Spirit we can do nothing. We do not even know how to speak to God in prayer, but in our weakness the Spirit comes to our aid.

The Spirit of God, which is the Spirit of the risen Christ, is at the same time the Spirit of the crucified Christ. 'The Spirit which inspires love that "seeks not its own" is the Spirit of Christ crucified, and the cross is its distinctive mark'.[5] In the life of the Church, the work of the Spirit is hidden. Karl Rahner puts it like this: 'The essential nature of genuine experience of the Spirit does not consist in particular objects of experience found in human awareness but occurs rather when a man experiences the radical re-ordering of his transcendent nature in knowledge and freedom towards the immediate reality of God through God's self-communication in grace.'[6] That is to say, the power of the Spirit corresponds to the hidden love of God which is everywhere at work, but which is not readily accessible to our normal criteria of success and progress. In the power of the Spirit the Church may fail where it hopes to succeed, and triumph where on the face of it it may be expected to fail.

We cannot use the Holy Spirit as an 'explanation' in theology, in the way that a scientific theory 'explains' certain phenomena, for even in its revelation in Christ the spiritual nature of God, in its complex reality as Father, Son and Spirit, remains infinitely mysterious to us. Yet this deeply mysterious presence *is* the Christian God, and no amount of theorising explanation, whether in shallow rationalisation or pious mystification, can alter the nature of this reality. We may find it helpful in thinking of God as a complex spiritual reality, as the ground of all our existence, to remember the imagery of St John's gospel, with its dynamic and moving identity between Father, Son and Spirit. The Father is present and at work in the Son, who in turn continues to be active and present in the Spirit. God invites us to worship him in Spirit and in truth by making himself accessible to us through his Son, and in the mission of his Spirit. Through the Spirit we, his creation, may respond, to the gift of grace in Jesus Christ. So the Spirit, as the Spirit of God, remains, as Karl Barth put it in a striking phrase, 'the most intimate friend of a proper human understanding of man',[7] man before God his creator and fulfilment.

The Spirit is present in the Church, not as a power at the disposal of churchmen but as the subject of the Church's obedience. Through the Spirit, the risen Christ makes himself present again in the Church and in the world. Through this presence of God as Spirit, and again almost contrary to all appearance, the Church which is so often the death of the gospel may be turned, so that the gospel is the life of the Church. In this way the Church may still be the instrument of Christ who is the life of the world.

3 The Church: The biblical foundation

THE BIBLE IN THE CHURCH

The Bible has been and is a powerful and wonderful force in human history. Through it the Christian gospel has been brought to multitudes. Life has been civilised in ways beyond the imagination of much humanist endeavour towards the civilisation of society. The peace of God through Jesus Christ has become an ultimate reality in the lives of millions of people. Where this force has been absent, a harsh and bitter inhumanity to man has been all too evident.

Christian societies have not themselves always handled this resource wisely. The Bible is the humiliation and scandal of the Church as well as its great asset. The gospel has an awkward way of breaking through wrong uses of the Bible and exposing their shallowness in devastating fashion. 'Both read the Bible day and night, but one reads black while the other reads white.' Both whites and blacks, to use a context not thought of by Alexander Pope in his couplet, have given notorious examples of how not to use the Bible. Needless to say, this applies equally to other focal points of Christian tradition, whether sacramental piety, church authority, social gospel or whatever.

We mentioned earlier the fact that different churches have used the Bible to reflect their own self-understanding through the ages, and indeed how the Bible reflects its own background. Such links between text and context need not obscure the search for objective truth. We have to be aware of the sorts of questions that we are asking as we ask them, so that we don't vote ourselves that complete and absolute objectivity and impartiality which we deny to others. In this way we may hope to achieve the maximum true objectivity in our analysis.

How is the Christian to tackle the biblical evidence in trying to make up his or her mind about the scriptural foundations of the

Church? This chapter will be no substitute for the number of excellent studies by biblical scholars listed at the end of this book, but I hope at least to indicate some of the central issues and some paths through the mass of conflicting theories. This variety of interpretation is indeed a central problem. Different scholars have gone about their task in different ways. Which is the correct method, and what happens if we choose the wrong path?

Clearly a central concern of the Church of Jesus Christ must be Jesus' own understanding of community and of human relation to God in community. Did Jesus intend to found the Church? If he did, what follows? If he did not, so what? What do such concepts as covenant, Kingdom of God, Messiah and the like tell us about Jesus and the Church? What about the Holy Spirit in all this?

ECCLĒSIA

Let me begin at a much less exalted level with a brief look at the word *ecclēsia*, which we might decently expect sometimes at least to mean something like the Church. Since we can't expect to produce theology straight out of dictionaries, we should perhaps look at some of the ways in which the word is used. In Acts (5:11; 8:1,3 etc.) *ecclēsia*, appears to mean a session of the people's assembly, so that won't get us very far. It would be nice if we could find a meaning with instant theological appeal, like 'called out of the world', but the New Testament doesn't appear to say so. However we do find in the Qumran scrolls reference to a community awaiting the coming of the Messiah at the end of time, and that may provide a better hint to the later New Testament use of the word *ecclēsia* as church. Certainly there were other sacred gatherings around, indicated by *ecclēsia* equal to *qahal* in the Septuagint, and by *synagōgē*, also in the Septuagint, and in the New Testament itself. The *synagōgē* understood itself as the true people of God in the Old Testament, but it is hard to find such a specific reference to *ecclēsia* in the New Testament until we come to the world of Ephesians and First Timothy. Whatever the earliest Christians were up to, they were certainly not writing learned essays in systematic theology. *Ecclēsia* is the congregation, even groups of congregations, but not necessarily always the true people of God in the Old Testament sense. New symbols were coming in, of the Church as the Body and as the House of God, and these helped Christians to understand themselves and their mission. These early congregations were not of course in a position to codify and rationalise their uses of various customs and terminologies. The result is that it is possible for later scholars and churches to set up their own patterns from the biblical building blocks in almost any shape they like.

In Acts the Christian congregations are already a definite force in society. Through them the Holy Spirit is at work. This is also the case in the Pauline writings and in John, in which the Church works under the guidance of the Paraclete. The Messiah of Israel is already on his heavenly throne, and through the Spirit is active in the Church. The Church is filled with the power of the Spirit. The gift of the Spirit in the Church is of course also present in Paul – cf. Galatians 2:20.

But if the Church was already part of the realm of the Spirit, how was it to cope with reconciling the different groups in its midst, of Jewish and Gentile background? For Paul, unity was to be found in Christ alone; hence the unifying metaphor of the body,[1] in later ages to be developed much further in reflection on the relations between Church and incarnation. Steps in this direction are provided by Ephesians and Colossians, and in a quite unique manner in Johannine reflection on Christology and discipleship, notably in the famous meditation on the vine and its branches.

In the earliest communities the Christians are themselves the Church. In time however the metaphors take on their own life, as it were, and the Christians are *in* the Church. The Church may come to stand over against the Christians. Scattered increasingly abroad, Christians began to find a new sense of unity of concept, a Church anticipating the future and soon even seen as pre-existent in God's plan of salvation. Such developments have sometimes been regarded as sinister fruits of institutionalism and sometimes that is what they become. But to see them in this way would not be to see them in their historical development.

THE PEOPLE OF GOD

There was then the *ecclēsia*, the new *ecclēsia* in place of the old, gradually working out the growing implications of what it would be in the future to be the true people of God. But the centre of the gospel and of the new *ecclēsia* was Jesus, at once the fulfilment and the transformation of the Old Testament expectation of the Messiah. A Messiah would come and save his people, and his people would be with him. Whatever the origins of the famous prophecy in Matthew 16:18 about the building of the Church, this clearly refers to the eschatological community of the Messiah. We shall have to return to Jesus and the Church. In his life on earth Jesus called his disciples. This may not yet be a formal gathering of those conscious of being the true people of God. This does not mean, as has sometimes been thought, that the Church was a kind of cover-up for disappointment caused by the failure of the parousia to occur after Jesus' death. On the contrary, the pictures of the Church in the New Testament are the grateful tributes of men and women whose lives have been transformed by the power of the risen Christ.

In order to be aware of the wider dimensions of the rich variety of the biblical material it is highly desirable to look at a study such as Paul Minear's splendid *Images of the Church*[2]. Minear analysed nearly a hundred of these images, grouped, apart from what he termed the minor images, round the four basic themes of the people of God, the new creation, the fellowship of faith and the body of Christ. So, for example, in considering the familiar image of the people of God, Minear explores its deep roots in the Old Testament. It was natural that many of the concepts used in the many strands of the Old Testament tradition concerning Israel should be used by Christians. Apart from the image of Israel itself, we find study of related images such as the sons of Abraham, the house of David, the remnant, the elect, a holy nation, the twelve tribes, and of the various strands of the Old Testament covenant traditions, which were understood to be fulfilled in the new. Minear's persuasive and, to my mind, highly successful presentation brings out the ways in which many patterns of metaphor and description concerning the Christian community come together in the biblical narratives. No single image or congregational situation can be regarded as normative for *the* doctrine of the Church. But together the various conceptions underline the centrality of concern with every aspect of the life of the community in Christian response to the gospel. As he puts it in a striking comparison, the New Testament conception of the Church is higher than that of any high church, for it is concerned with the love of God in Christ and the exaltation of the community and of humanity in God, and is at the same time lower than any low church doctrine, for it is concerned with God's self-humiliation in identification with the darkest aspects of the created world.

JESUS AND THE CHURCH

We must return now to the relation of Jesus to the Church, and to the historical circumstances concerning Jesus of Nazareth in the first instance.

It is worth recalling that the first chapter of the most scholarly and reliable life of Jesus in our time begins with the confession that no one is any longer in a position to write a life of Jesus.[3] More recent attempts to interpret the historical evidence by appeal to the 'voice' of Jesus as an authority for theological programmes do not appear to have been entirely successful. However, though we are far short of the requirements for an exhaustive or definitive biography, it would be equally inaccurate to say that we know nothing of Jesus. We know that he was a Jew of the male sex who lived in the Middle East. We know when he lived and we know quite a lot about his social and cultural background. From his actions, his associates and the general directions of his life we gain knowledge of the sort of person he was. Most important for his mission in life, he was a religious man, devoted to God and to his fellow men. He clashed with church and state, with religion and politics. He taught, and his teaching was important to him. He taught the impending arrival of the Kingdom of God. There was a connection between his teaching, his person even, and the Kingdom. He taught mainly, though not invariably, through parables, often concerning that Kingdom. Much of his teaching and authority were indirect, allusive. He was condemned as a traitor in circumstances which still remain obscure, and he died as a common criminal. This man, and no other, is at the centre of the life and worship of the Church, and this fact ought to have central significance for any doctrine of the Church.

Jesus worshipped Israel's God. He appears to have seen in his own mission both the fulfilment and the radical transformation of messianic and covenant expectations. Nevertheless he died, like all other men. What happened afterwards is the witness not of Jesus but of his followers, and is of crucial importance for understanding his significance. But I return here to the man in history.

Jesus was and remains the focal point and source of Christianity, and for Christians after the Resurrection there is a sense in which the life and work of Jesus is superseded because the background against which it took place is transformed. Yet there is also an important continuity, for the risen Christ is the same as the one who was the earthly Jesus. Jesus was concerned with the coming Kingdom of God. In the material represented by the Sermon on the Mount he indicated, using traditional Jewish theology, something of the quality of the Kingdom and the attitudes to God and man which its coming would imply. This was an eschatological kingdom, but here too there was a continuity of standards before and after. Jesus appears to have envisaged the near arrival of the eschaton. Nevertheless he was familiar with the community life, sacred and secular, of Judaism, and indeed entered into this. He had his own followers, and he may even have been familiar with institutional structures among other groups, of the sort represented in some of the Qumran communities. He appears to have been conscious of his own role as a focus of the activity of God's kingdom. As Christians, confessing God's unique involvement in his life, we can scarcely expect complete illumination of the deepest mystery in the universe.

Historical research seems to indicate that Jesus linked the sayings about the Kingdom to a fund of material about the messianic Son of man. Sayings about the Kingdom of God and Son of man appear to be linked only in early Christian material. It may be that Jesus saw himself as the coming Son, or that he related his mission to that of the Son of man in relation to the kingdom. Again the focal points are stress on the grace of God, on devotion to God and on the welfare of men, especially the poor and the oppressed.[4]

We do not know exactly what Jesus thought about the messianic kingdom, but we know that he regarded it as the fulfilment of God's creation for all men. His followers were to seek that kingdom and to help men in their search for it. His own authority was indirect, and he pointed not to himself but to his father in heaven.

Despite the complexities of historical explanation, we should now be able to begin to build up a coherent picture of the biblical foundation. In the Old Testament Israel's developing consciousness of its role in history as the particular people of God was focussed in ideas of the covenant and the remnant which was to be the basis of a new convenant. God had made a covenant with Israel at Sinai. He had chosen this people in order to make his name known over all the earth. Disobedience in Israel brought prophetic warnings of punishment, and at the same time promise of a new covenant for the remnant of the faithful. From this promise came the Messianic hope of the Redeemer, who would come at the end of the age to fulfil his mission by gathering around him the faithful remnant.

Jesus comes through the gospel narratives as one who understands his mission within the framework of expectation in Israel. In his teaching and action he proclaims the coming of God's kingdom, whose inauguration is linked to response in his own person. He offers forgiveness of sins, and in his words and action he confirms and at the same time radically transforms the law of Israel. He is crucified, and his followers are scattered.

In the *ecclēsia* the continuing experience of the forgiving grace of God is linked to the resurrection of the crucified Jesus. There is growing awareness that through the life, death and resurrection of Jesus the new creation has begun, the covenant is fulfilled, through the Spirit of the risen Christ God is experienced as presence in a new way in the life of the *ecclēsia*. The community confesses Jesus as Christ and Lord, recognises God's gift of the Spirit in baptism, gathers in the presence of the Spirit at the Lord's supper, understands its mission as the people of God in many different parts of the Mediterranean world.

ST PAUL

In St Paul the phraseology about the Kingdom and the Son has largely disappeared. As in the relationship between the Son and the Remnant in Daniel, the community is now inseparable from its leader who is its head and embodiment. From the focal point of the cross from which the son of man has been vindicated, the Kingdom of God must advance, through death to life.

In the period between the times, Paul feels able to believe that Jesus is Lord and to say 'I, yet not I'. The spiritual presence of Christ is at once an annihilation and a renewal of the self. Paul characteristically expresses this Christian consciousness of faith, at personal and community level, in the language of justification and sanctification.

St Paul speaks of the Church as both the individual congregation and the whole people of God. There are particular churches at Corinth (1 Cor. 1:2) and in other provinces (Gal. 1:22; Rom. 16:1.

etc.). All are individual manifestations of the greater Church (1 Cor. 7:17), whether they are full congregations or simply house churches (1 Cor. 16:19). Paul's characteristic expression to describe and emphasise the unity of the Church is of course the body. The Church forms one body (1 Cor. 12:12f; Rom. 12:5f) whose head is Christ. The faithful are the members of the body (Col. 1:2,24; Eph. 1:22–3). Through the Church, Christ is present and active in the world now. When the Church comes together for worship Christ is present, in the preaching of the gospel and in the celebration of the Lord's Supper (1 Cor. 10:16f). The Church, which is the body of Christ, is at the same time the Israel of God, in whom all the promises of the Old Testament are transformed and fulfilled.

The image of the body expresses both the close identification of Christ with his people and the spiritual unity of the members of the body. It refers to the internal life of the Church rather than to the relation of Christ to all mankind. There is of course no reason why we should not look on the body as an image appropriate also to the eschatological fulfilment of the firstfruits begun in the Church, when Christ shall be all in all.

As in the rest of the New Testament, we shall not appreciate the full scope of St Paul's thought simply by looking at the images directly related to the community. It is as the Church of God that the Church is the basis of the new creation. It is in the light of the life, death and resurrection of Christ that the ongoing life of the community, its participation in and solidarity with suffering, its endurance through and beyond death, its universal significance for all mankind is to be understood. As in Adam all die, so in Christ new life is brought to all men. The Church is the centre of the new Israel, the scene of the working of the Spirit of the risen Christ.

THE NEW TESTAMENT PICTURE

A very similar account of the relation of the Christian to God and his fellow Christians is given in the Johannine writings, in terms of discipleship. In the parable of the vine, there can be no Christianity in individual or community apart from the constant renewing power of God. As Bultmann puts it, 'The commitment that is required of us is not, basically, a continued being *for*, but a being *from*. It is not taking up a position, but an allowing of ourselves to be held, as the branch is supported by the vine.'[5]

The Johannine Christ is the true shepherd of his flock. He prays not simply for the disciples whom the Father has given him, but for those who will be led to the faith by the apostles. He prays that all who believe may be one, as the Father and the Son are one. (John 17:20–23). He wills to draw all men to himself (John 12:32).

In other areas of the New Testament we find fresh imagery concerning the centrality and the nature of the community. In the letter to the Hebrews, the 'wandering people of God', who are not tied to particular places but are always on the move, and always in the presence of the Spirit, the Church is the community of those who are bound together by the gift of faith, led by faith to strike out in new directions.

In Ephesians[6] the first keynote is thanksgiving, gratitude for the salvation of the community through Christ and in Christ. Past dissensions are blotted out in the forgiveness of sins. In Christ Jews and Gentiles are reconciled, through the peace of God. 'Thus you are no longer aliens in a foreign land, but fellow citizens with God's people, members of God's household. You are built upon the foundation laid by the apostles and prophets, and Jesus Christ himself is the chief foundation stone' (2:19–20, NEB). The secret of the gospel is the reconciliation which Christ brings. So Paul prays for the continuation of faith in this gospel within the community.

Within the community there are different sorts of gifts of service, for the building up of the body of Christ. Conduct must be related to belief. 'Be generous to one another, tender hearted, forgiving one another as God in Christ forgave you' (Eph. 4:32). Beyond this, Christian service includes the duty of intercessory prayer. It is entirely consistent that the letter should then end in benediction. 'Peace to the brotherhood and love, with faith, from God the Father and the Lord Jesus Christ. God's grace be with all who love our Lord Jesus Christ, ... grace and immortality.' Prayer and the answer to prayer is of the essence of the community.

In thinking of the doctrine of the Church in the present we shall not wish simply to refurbish the New Testament images. We do not live in the first century AD. Yet because we are inevitably prone to modernising the biblical pictures it is always refreshing to think them through again and to rediscover a world which, precisely in its strangeness from our own modern environment, may throw a powerful light on the question of the nature of Christian discipleship in the Church today.

It is easy to take 'the biblical witness' for granted. Yet if we have eyes to see, it has been and may still be a profoundly exciting and enormously varied stimulus to fresh thinking about the nature of the Church and of its service in the name of its Lord to which the narratives bear testimony.

4 The test of history

THE PATRISTIC WITNESS

In the New Testament we read of the true people of God, gathered in community in the service of the resurrected Lord. This understanding continues to guide the thought of the congregations described slightly later in the second century by the so-called Apostolic Fathers, for example in such writings as the *Didache* and the *Shepherd of Hermas*. Whereas these pictures emphasise the goodness of the lives of community members and their moral purity, following the stress on morality characteristic of the theology of the period, the letters of Ignatius, Bishop in Asia Minor, take up and carry further the Johannine teaching on the links between the exalted Christ and his body on earth, even to the extent of seeing the customs of the churches on earth as copies of the heavenly order of the angels. Now the pre-existence of the Church, corresponding to the pre-existence of its Lord, is stressed. Here we might to some extent see, with all due caution, in a second-century world the main streams of later Protestant moral earnestness and Catholic mysticism developing, with their particular strengths and attendant weaknesses.[1]

This is of course a selective picture. Even in the New Testament period there were great diversities of belief and practice in the various congregations. After all, many Christian congregations, e.g. in Edessa and Egypt, were so heterodox by that standard at the time of the putting together of the New Testament canon that they were simply excluded from mention. This was particularly the case in congregations with a strong tendency to Gnosticism, i.e., especially a minimising of the importance of the historical life, activity and death of Jesus.[2]

The New Testament material was reconsidered in important ways by Irenaeus, the greatest Christian thinker of the early period, in a careful restatement of all the main strands of Christian doctrine. The

Church for *Irenaeus* (*c.* AD 130–200), as for Ignatius and Paul, is the mystical body of Christ. Against the Gnostics who wanted to spirtualise the gospel into a series of ideas and mysteries rather than a witness in history to God's particular action through the death and resurrection of Jesus Christ, Irenaeus was deeply concerned to relate spirit to action, spiritual community to historical community.

'In the Church God has instituted Apostles, prophets and teachers, together with all the rest of the power of the Spirit. Those who do not participate in this are not part of the Church. For where the Church is, there is also the spirit of God, and where the spirit of God is, there is also the Church and all grace' (*Against the Heretics*, 3:24.1).

This development is carried further in the fascinating imagery of Irenaeus' pupil *Hippolytus*, for whom the Church is at one time paradise on earth, and at another the ark afloat in the world and rescuing the faithful remnant from manifold disaster. The image of the Church as a ship afloat on the stormy waters of the world is one which travels down the ages and recurs in the symbol of the ship and the cross of the World Council of Churches. It is a somewhat ambiguous symbol. It may suggest a brave voyage of mission across the perilousness of opposition. It may also suggest a battening down of the hatches against the world on the part of a smug and self-preserving élite – indeed a parable of the Church's glory and its misery. Corresponding to this image of being on the move, Hippolytus' Church lives spiritually in heaven, and the earth is but the scene of its temporary visitation.

The biblical contrast between things on earth and things in heaven was given a tremendous boost by the work of *Origen* (*c.* AD 185–254), the most powerful intellect in the ancient Church. The informal differentiations of the biblical imagery were now to be developed systematically through the potent philosophical tools of Neoplatonism. We must be careful here not to suggest a complete divorce in principle between biblical and later Greek thought. There was a constant interpenetration between Greek and Semitic thought in the Near East from at least the seventh century BC. What we see now is not the inauguration but the speeding up and rationalisation of this progress. This did not mean, either, that the gospel disappears in favour of the Academy. Origen was opposed to nothing more than to Gnosticism, and was a confessor who suffered for the Church. The fact remains that he marks another significant and in some ways fateful turning point in the Church's understanding of itself. Now there are ordinary Christians and a spiritual élite of the perfect, differentiated constitutionally. There are orders of spiritual being in the Church on earth, corresponding to orders in the Church in heaven among the angels. This concept of the Church as a heavenly community is basic to the understanding of the Eastern Church in the Byzantine period.

In the West it was not so much the spiritual and eschatological as the institutional and legal aspects of the Church which came to assume a new importance. *Cyprian* in North Africa stressed the centrality of the ministry. The Church is the source of salvation. As he puts it in a famous phrase: there is no salvation outside the Church. Political and other conflicts brought out inherent tensions in the understanding of the Church. The ordained ministers were central. Did their centrality depend on their office as such or upon their personal moral purity? The followers of the African theologian *Donatus* thought the latter. Bitter dissension led to schism.[3]

AUGUSTINE TO AQUINAS

The decisive influence on Western understanding of the Church, as indeed of much else in Christianity for a thousand years, was *Augustine* (AD 354–430). The Church for him is first and foremost the community of those who love God. *Amor Dei*, the love of God, is the centre. Love and do what you like is the watchword – though what counted as love was to be strictly circumscribed in the discipline of the Church. To the extent that it is a faithful participant in the Kingdom of Christ the Church is the city of God.[4] At the same time the historical Church is a mixed body, including both the good and (against the Donatists) the less good. The historical Church has within it an invisible core of the faithful people of God. But only God can say who within the body belongs to the true elect, the '*congregatio sanctorum*'. This core validates the divine authority of the Church. Augustine, the former professor of rhetoric, could put it as strongly as this. 'In fact, I should not have believed the gospel, had not the authority of the Catholic church compelled me to do so.'

The heritage of Augustine could lead in many directions. In some cases it seemed to point to the centrality of inner spirituality and personal practice of spiritual love. In other cases it led to new stress on the external criteria of the authority of the Church as an institution and of its officers.

The Church's claims to authority in this world and indeed in the next world constantly increased. In the famous Papal Bull *Unam Sanctam* of 1302 it is claimed that the invisible Church is completely identified with the sacramental institutions of the visible Church, so that the visible Church as an historical institution has unlimited control over both spiritual and temporal matters. Such claims did not of course endear the Church to temporal rulers, kings and emperors. They also provoked protest from the ranks of the theologians. *Wyclif* (*c*.1329–84) recalled the institutional Church to the community of the disciples. Combining Franciscan simplicity with national aspirations, he stimulated response throughout Europe. The development of the spiritual and mystical side of Augustine brought as always a further threat to the churches as institutions. Where there is free access to personal communion with God through mystical experience, sacramental apparatus begins to appear superfluous. It was part of the great service of *Thomas Aquinas* (*c*. 1225–74) to the institutional Church in the middle ages that he combined the mystical tradition with the ordinances of the Church, in an intellectually convincing synthesis deriving from a critical reappraisal of Aristotle's philosophy.

REFORMATION

The Reformation constitutes a great watershed in the history of the Church. After being overstressed for centuries, this fact is now sometimes under-estimated in thinking about the Church. It is of course true that Luther drew extensively on the heritage of the later middle ages. It is equally true that there was to be another great watershed between the ancient and the modern world in the divide of the Enlightenment. Having said this, the impact of the whole complex phenomenon of the Reformation was colossal, and remains so in the modern world.

Following Augustine, *Luther* (1483–1546)[5] stressed the invisibility of the Church. The Church is the spiritual, eternal city of God, in existence since the beginning of the world, whose head is Jesus Christ. The Church is present wherever faith receives the word of God and the Holy Spirit gathers the faithful into congregations.

The Church is the creature of the gospel. It stands under the cross. The true Church is hidden. This is basic. External appearances of the Church are ambiguous and full of inadequacies. The Church stands beside earthly institutions. It is not however a similar, parallel institution, but a community of people in personal relationship. There are two kingdoms, of the church and of the world. Each has its role in creation as God's order for mankind. Basic to Luther's understanding of the community of the faithful under the cross is his doctrine of justification by faith alone.

Luther's work was to be developed further in classical form by *Calvin* (1509–64).[6] Because of the rivalries of Calvinist and Lutheran theologians and confessions in later periods, it is generally forgotten that Calvin was in crucial respects a Lutheran as much as a Calvinist, if indeed he can be called the latter. (Aristotle, after all, was the first and greatest Platonist, even if his own school was to develop in characteristic and distinctive directions!) For Calvin there were two main marks of the Church. The Church is where the word of God is truly preached and the sacraments are correctly administered. To these he added a third, secondary but still integral mark: ecclesiastical discipline, properly directed. This third aspect was to achieve much greater theoretical prominence in the thought of his successors than in Calvin himself, for whom it was more a practical than a theoretical measure. Calvin stressed again the visible face of the Church. *Zwingli* was to return to part of the medieval tradition, and the invisible remnant in the larger gathering.

The real heirs of the mystical tradition of the free religious spirit were the various sections of the Baptist movement. These were the Protestant heirs of St Francis, and their reward was to be continued persecution by both the great Churches, of reformation and counter-reformation. Where the pursuit of God as an individual spiritual rather than a communal experience was pursued in an intellectual sphere, we find not Baptist but spiritualist groups. These flourished in the movement of German pietism focussed on the thought of *P. J. Spener* and led to *Zinzendorf* (1700–60) and the Moravian Brethren, with a renewal of the ideals of the Brethren of the Common Life of later medieval times.

ENLIGHTENMENT

With the great theologian *F. D. E. Schleiermacher* (1768–1834) we see a coming together of the official and unofficial Protestant traditions, the state church and Moravian piety, on the other side of the great divide, the Enlightenment. For Schleiermacher the Church is the community of those for whom the feeling of absolute dependence on God is the centre of their understanding of reality, and for whom Jesus Christ is the lens or focus of that understanding of God and his redemption. The institutional Church is to be ur ierstood as the servant of society. In order to focus on Jesus Christ as the centre of redemption the old confessional differences dating from pre-enlightenment thought must be set aside. It was typical of Schleiermacher that in addition to his intellectual understanding of the centrality of the Church to Christianity, there was an intensive practical effort to produce unions between the Reformed and Lutheran confessions in Germany. For Schleiermacher, to be a modern theologian was at the same time to be an active Churchman. Christianity was a commitment not to a romantic symbol or idea but to a community of Christians working in the wider community of modern society.

A rather more radical understanding of the world, God's creation, as itself the Church, was developed by *Richard Rothe*, anticipating by a hundred years much of the 'secular Christianity' of our own time. Schleiermacher's work was carried on by *Albrecht Ritschl* (1822–89) who saw all human ethical activity as potentially contributing to and anticipating the coming Kingdom of God. The catastrophes of the twentieth century produced in turn disenchantment with the world and its progress. Against the pressure of Nazism *Karl Barth* (1886–1968) became the chief architect of what was perhaps *the* characteristic Protestant confession of our time, the Barmen Declaration. Here again, as at the Reformation, the Church is the 'community of brothers, in which Jesus Christ is at work through the Holy Spirit in Word and Sacrament'.[7]

FURTHER DEVELOPMENT

In Catholic Europe Reformation brought Counter-Reformation, and a hardening of positions all round. The theology of the Church at the Council of Trent (1545–63) was a defensive product of the fortress mentality, designed for negative rather than positive results. Such attempts at mediating theologies as the ingenious work of Cardinal Contarini were brushed aside. Again the true Church is identical with the structure of the Roman Catholic Church. Stress is laid on the institutional ministry and especially on its hierarchical structure. This ecclesiology was finally sealed and perfected at the First Vatican Council of 1870. Now the infallibility of the Pope, albeit under certain limited conditions, was finally held to be binding on all Catholics. Opposition to official positions was ruthlessly stifled. The Catholic Modernists, emerging thirty years later, were to lose their battles and themselves pay the penalty of being in permanent and debilitated opposition. Thus Tridentine Catholicism triumphed.

It would of course be quite misleading to see all Catholic Christianity from Trent to the first Vatican Council as simply a sterile preoccupation with authoritarian ecclesiology. The magnificence of baroque culture in painting, architecture and music, the great flourishing of romantic literature, the continuing stream of mystical prayer and piety, the development of social action and many other dimensions bear witness to the continuing stream of unbroken Catholic piety enriching European life. Where rules are inhibiting, human ingenuity often contrives to find new outlets for creativity. But the results for theology and the Church were undoubtedly often stultifying. Since the second world war however the face of Catholic theology and Church has changed, at first slowly and then with increasing rapidity. These changes are canonised in the declarations of the second Vatican Council and in the movements towards complete reconsideration of Church, ministry and sacraments that have followed. In some ways the pace of change in Catholic circles has been faster than in Protestant Christianity. Nothing today, it seems, can be taken for granted, and nothing need be quite as it seems.

The other great development of the Church in modern times has been the growth of the ecumenical movement. Membership of the World Council of Churches is open to all churches which 'recognise our Lord Jesus Christ as God and Saviour'. Through a series of world conferences the WCC has generated a vast literature on Christian thought and practice, and in the process has over the years formed and reformed a large number of different doctrines of the Church. The danger of ecumenism is the constant danger of introspection and preciosity. Though creative tensions are always healthy, the uncreative tensions and mutually disparaging attitudes among the churches are certainly no aid towards the service of Jesus Christ in his world.

5 The Church now: Moltmann, Küng and Ramsey

SELECTING VOICES

We have looked at the Church in the past. What are we to make of the Church in the present? I am tempted to ask, what are we to make of the Church in the future? But it is too easy to speak of the past and the future and to say nothing of the present. The grounds for future hope are in the present if anywhere. A faith which is founded simply on past promises and future aspirations is a pale shadow of the good news of the New Testament gospel. *Hic et nunc*: what of God's presence right now?

In tackling the question of the present we shall look at approaches to the doctrine of the Church in three contemporary theologians. All are different, yet together they reflect some of the most significant elements in the question of the Church in our time. They are neither completely comprehensive nor completely representative. But I hope they may open up the issues in a constructive way. I have chosen to look at the Church in the thought of *Jürgen Moltmann* (b.1926), *Hans Küng* (b.1928) and *Michael Ramsey* (b.1904). This is not a list of the top theologians of the age. Bultmann and Bonhoeffer, Barth, Rahner and Pannenberg, the Niebuhr brothers and others who have had important things to say about the Church will appear in our narrative. But to enlarge the list would simply duplicate the analysis.

Moltmann is a somewhat distinctive sort of Protestant, and Küng is a rather Protestant Catholic. Behind both stands the figure of Karl Barth, at once the most controversial and the most significant theologian of this century.[1] However one may judge his specific theological proposals, Barth was a man of quite astonishing gifts of character and intellect. He never gave way to the temptation to follow fashion for its own sake. He was above all his own man. That is why, though he has suffered from the imitations of followers who have exhibited the universal failings of party hacks, his own work still commands the careful attention of professional theologians, and is taken forward in a flexible and critical manner in the hands of such independent thinkers as Moltmann and Küng. In Moltmann's ecclesiology the connections with Barth are particularly close. But they are given a new and contemporary application to the political, economic and cultural problems of the secular world.

JÜRGEN MOLTMANN

Moltmann's main contribution to the understanding of the Church is found in his book, *The Church in the Power of the Spirit*. We noted earlier that popular images of the Church are often scarcely flattering. Moltmann's Church is far removed from all such faint-hearted speculation. As he puts it on the first page of his work, 'The Church is the people of God and will give an account of itself at all times to the God who has called it into being, liberated it and gathered it'. This reaffirmation and exposition of biblical imagery concerning the Church runs through the book, and is a source at once of strength and weakness.

In a chapter on the dimensions of a doctrine of the Church today Moltmann speaks of the need for the inner renewal of the Church by the Spirit of Christ, who is the power of the coming kingdom. He underlines the importance of the movements of the World Council of Churches towards a Christological ecclesiology, i.e. basing our understanding of the Church on our understanding of Christ, and then goes on to consider the Church in history as participating in the history of God. He then turns to the relations of the earthly and the risen Jesus to the Church. Liberated from Godforsakenness through the loneliness of Jesus on the cross, the Church becomes the Church of the Kingdom of God. This has implications for dialogue with other faiths, and for matters of human rights and political practice.

The Church is the servant of the hidden work of the Spirit or else it is nothing. The Church is not only concerned however with human rights and political practice. The history of the Church has at its centre the preaching of the gospel, the practice of pastoral care and the administration of the sacraments within the life of the worshipping community. The argument of this section is summarised in four points, but these scarcely do justice to the foregoing material. Moltmann finally considers the marks of the

Church, one, holy, catholic and apostolic. 'Unity in freedom, holiness in poverty, catholicity in partisan support for the weak, and apostolate in suffering are the marks by which it is known in the world.'

We may look now at Moltmann's construction in more detail. What is distinctive, and why? Moltmann's is a thoroughly evangelical doctrine of the Church, in the true sense. He is passionately concerned with faithfulness to the gospel of the biblical witness, and with its impact on the realities of the secular world in which we live, in all the various dimensions of culture and society on this planet. There is nothing inhibited about Moltmann's programme, nothing precious or parochial. He is concerned with the centre of the Christian gospel in the centre of human society. He is not concerned with pious huddles, liturgical limbos, religious nationalism, transcendental humanism or any other substitute for the service of the gospel. As such he stands firmly in the best tradition of Christian thought from Augustine and Thomas to Luther and Barth.

Moltmann is concerned with a Church which is the Church of Jesus Christ. It is the Church of God, Father, Son and Spirit, whose operation within the Church is its sole legitimation.

At the same time the Church is a missionary, ecumenical and even political Church. It is not simply a reflection of European culture and interests but must be engaged with the concerns of the whole human family in all their agonies, conflicts and contradictions. In such engagement the church participates in the history of God himself, since in Jesus God has related himself in a new way to human history. There is a section on the biblical witness to Jesus and his messianic mission, and a long section on what it is to be the Church of the Kingdom of God today. Moltmann then deals with sacraments and ministry in speaking of the Church in the presence and in the power of the Holy Spirit. There follows the restatement of the marks of the true Church.

Jesus is the one who offers open friendship in community, and who as the resurrected Lord sustains life through death, bringing hope and salvation to the poor, the oppressed and the socially disadvantaged in every society. What emerges is something like a reaffirmation of the Franciscan ideal in Schleiermacher's modern urban community – apostolic poverty understood in the complex structures of today's world. The strengths and weaknesses of this theology of the Church are very similar to those of Moltmann's magnificent study in Christology, *The Crucified God*. There is too a very necessary and brilliantly developed affirmation and exposition of the substantive issues of our faith in Jesus Christ, and in the Church; there is little in the way of explanation of the issues which puzzle those outside or on the edges of faith, as they look at the ambiguities of our Church practice and the puzzles raised by our easy use of familiar Christian imagery.

HANS KÜNG

'For about two hundred years the Protestant Church has largely ceased to be interesting', wrote Karl Barth in 1932. If you want a good illustration of the exciting and imaginative challenge of Catholic theology, then the work of Hans Küng is an excellent example. Yet paradoxically, Küng is in some ways the most Protestant of Catholic theologians.

We noticed that Küng, like Moltmann, and indeed many others who have produced significant theology in the last half of this century, was at one time a pupil of Karl Barth and was deeply influenced by him. This comes through strongly, not only in his fascinating work on justification, in which he argued that there was no vital difference between Barth's understanding of justification and that of the best Catholic tradition, but also in the numerous books which deal with the church. We mentioned the similarity to Moltmann, deriving from Barth. But there are also differences, from which we may learn quite a lot about constructing doctrines of the Church.

Hans Küng has written numerous books on the Church and related issues. We may look here at his major work *The Church*. Küng begins characteristically with a section devoted to the Church in the present. The real essence of the Church must not be divorced from its historical form, but is expressed in its historical form.[2] The theological expression of the Church's image is variously expressed at different stages in its history and indeed in the diverse images of the New Testament. The image is often distorted by the appearance of the Church as a contradiction of its own declared mission.

What then is the origin and basis of the Church? Jesus preached about the reign of God, which is near in the presence of Jesus' own person. We live in the period between the times of inauguration and fulfilment. Jesus did not found the Church, but in his ministry laid the foundations which bear fruit through faith in the Resurrection. The *ecclēsia* as congregation, community and church acts in the service of the coming reign of God, while not itself being identical with this. What then is the fundamental structure of the Church? The Church is the people of God, in historical and theological continuity with the Jewish people in the Old Testament and beyond. It is also the creation of the Spirit and the Church of the Spirit, manifesting charismatic dimensions. It is, too, the body of Christ. Through baptism its members are received into the body of Christ and are united, at local and universal level, in the fellowship of the Lord's Supper.

The dimensions of the Church are spelled out in the four traditional attributes. The Church is one, a unity in diversity which should lead to the reunion of the churches. The Church is Catholic, in an inclusive rather than an exclusive sense. The Church is holy, and yet sinful, forgiveness and renewal being constantly continuing aspects of the life of the Church. The Church is apostolic, in succession to the original community of the disciples.

Küng then turns to the offices of the Church, in two highly characteristic sections. First he stresses the priesthood of all believers. Christ is the only high priest and mediator, and there is a royal priesthood of all Christians. Ecclesiastical office is above all ministry. Service is the imitation of Christ, and it is to that service that the Petrine power and the Petrine ministry must be shaped. The Church is a pilgrim Church which sometimes falters and even appears on occasion to have no future. But it has not only a future but *the* future, the future of the Kingdom of God.

The similarities with Moltmann here are remarkable. Again the accent is on the Church as entirely dependent on the true service of Jesus Christ, on the pilgrim people of God walking towards God's future and in so doing serving the world in all its colourful and conflicting pluriformity. In both cases the stress is on the openness, the inclusive rather the exclusive nature of the Church, and on the body of Christ, not as a fortress of those who possess grace, but as a body of those who are constantly dependent on God's grace, who are given love only to pour it out in service for others, within and outside the community.

Whereas Küng is more concerned here with the issues of

intellectual freedom and the European cultural tradition, Moltmann speaks more consciously of freedom in the political and economic tensions of the rest of the world.

This latter, more universal perspective dominates much of Küng's later work, and is reflected in his treatment of the Church. The Church of *On Being a Christian* is above all a community of liberty, equality and fraternity. The Church itself should be both a place of equality of rights and an advocate of equality of rights in the world. What matters is not the exclusivity of Catholic or Protestant but the cause of Jesus Christ. This is a cause to be pursued through despair and indifference in constant hope. 'To be a Christian leads to the humanisation of mankind through the gospel of Jesus Christ.'

Küng has written on infallibility, and like all of us who think and write about theology he is not himself infallible. One of the most interesting constructive criticisms of his work, both in *The Church* and *On Being a Christian* comes from another Catholic theologian of our time, Karl Rahner. Küng, in thinking about man in community, reconsiders the old patristic notion of divinisation, and asks whether any modern man would care to be deified. He is, rightly, anxious to stress full commitment to the humanisation of man, and the freeing of the Church from past authoritarian pretensions, in which she has identified her own vested interests and prejudices with the authority of the Holy Spirit. The New Testament, says Rahner, speaks not only of the humanisation of man but of the gift of the Spirit and of God's immediate presence to men in self-giving.[3] It is for God, and only then for man, that man is to live. Though of course we would not wish, even eschatologically, simply to be submerged in the divine all, yet the grace of God and of his spiritual presence is prior to all our human commitment. Küng would be the last to deny this. But in practice he may not lay sufficient stress on the divine dimension of the church as, despite its manifold failings, the instrument of God's spirit. The Church is the Church of the crucified and risen Christ, as much as of the followers of Jesus of Nazareth. The one dimension arises from the other. Concern for a new understanding of spirit and spirituality runs through Rahner's work, and is seen as part of the future shape of the Church as a democratised and socio-critical Church.

The last word in this section must be allowed to Küng himself, who sees the danger of splitting hairs on conceptual models where no concrete progress is made. He sees this as the most dangerous contemporary threat to the move towards reunion of the churches. 'In all the churches, we have come to the point of ecumenical no-return! We can refuse to go forward; we can drift aimlessly and ultimately dry up; but to go back is impossible. Well then?'

MICHAEL RAMSEY

When Küng had completed his epoch-making volume on *The Church* he decided to dedicate the English edition to A. M. Ramsey, then Archbishop of Canterbury, with the comment that 'This will record my humble hope that there lies within the pages of this book a theological basis for a rapprochement between the churches of Rome and Canterbury.' Ramsey will provide our third perspective on the Church.

Turning from Moltmann and Küng to Ramsey appears on the face of it to be a clear-cut case of 'Backwards, Christian soldiers', a refusal to face the realities of the contemporary world. We move from the problems of political freedom in Latin America and of academic freedom in the European universities to the world of cloistered leisure and croquet on the archbishop's lawn. Appearances even here can be mildly deceptive. We may pause to reflect that the measured reasonableness of much Anglican theology has at least prevented it from endorsing either Nazi holocausts or other apolcalyptic idiocies fashionable in our time. In our liberated society, too, even archbishops can get themselves machine-gunned.

In moving from Moltmann and Küng to Ramsey we appear to turn from the university to the Church. But Moltmann and Küng are passionately committed to the Church, and Ramsey spent much of his life as a professor of theology. I want to begin with the book which made Ramsey a name as a theologian, *The Gospel and the Catholic Church*, published in 1936. This may seem a little unfair, since much has happened since then. But though we shall come across important modifications in his later thought, there are features still highly characteristic of Ramsey and of Anglican ecclesiology in this classic study. The keynote is the conviction set out on the first page of the preface.

The underlying conviction of this book is that the meaning of the Christian Church becomes most clear when it is studied in terms of the death and resurrection of Jesus Christ. . . . The doctrine of the Church is thus to be found within the Christian's knowledge of Christ crucified.

The key ideas of the book are easily sketched, though the quality of the presentation is not. The Church is the body of Christ crucified and risen. This approach is demanded by theology, by the reunion movements where Catholic order needs explaining not legalistically but in terms of the gospel, and by the implications for social reform. One man, Jesus Christ, has died for all, and therefore all share his death. Membership of the Church means death to self, and dependence on the one body. From the structure of the Church, catholic and apostolic, men may learn to share in Christ's death and in the universal family wherein Christ is made complete. The Church structure of bishops, presbytery and people still expresses the gospel of death and resurrection. The episcopate represents the general life of the Church beyond individuals and individual congregations, and is in that sense the *esse* of the universal Church.

The chapters devoted to liturgy and eucharist we shall consider later. Ramsey goes on to reflect on the truth of God, and the history of the Church in the Fathers, the Middle Ages and the Reformers, before finding in the *ecclēsia Anglicana* an 'essential unity of catholic and evangelical facts'. The underlying unity is illustrated from F. D. Maurice – a feature for which he has often been criticised. This brings back the question of reunion. Unity is to be sought not in terms of humanism but on the basis of Christ's death and resurrection, through which the origin, history and hopes of the Church are to be understood.

In time Ramsey's thought was to develop in various directions, notably in a much more flexible attitude to ecclesiology. Speaking at the inauguration of the federation of theological colleges in Cambridge he could speak of the 'blunder' of the General Synod of the Church of England in turning down the scheme of reunion with the Methodist Church, and raise questions about Establishment: 'It is inconceivable that Free Churchmen would join in a united Church which did not choose its own chief pastors, and if we Anglicans are serious about unity we shall not delay in facing this issue.'[4]

Speaking of his first book, he has said that he would not see 'structure' as a keynote of Church today, but would think rather of a number of complementary metaphors. Though hardly a 'political theologian' he was not afraid to call for the strongest measures in opposition to racism. He could condemn the death penalty at home as firmly as oppression abroad.

In *The Gospel and the Catholic Church* there is a strong emphasis on biblical theology, which he certainly never retracted. But Ramsey could see that sticking to the letter could kill the spirit. 'We can be sound in the theology of the Bible . . . Yet our biblical Theology can be held in a kind of vacuum, without sensitivity to the human context in which theology comes alive.'[5]

Having surveyed these three contemporary voices it is tempting to draw together a doctrine of the Church now at this point. However, since we cannot really consider the Church without the ministry and the sacraments, or the latter without the former, I should like now to go straight on to consideration, first of the ministry within the Church and then of the sacraments.

6 The Christian ministry

FORMS OF MINISTRY

It has long been customary for theologians to speak of 'Church, ministry and sacraments' in a single phrase, in that order, and we shall do the same. But we may think that in some ways, 'Church, sacraments and ministry' would be a better order. For the Church is the Church on the basis of its faithfulness to the gospel of word and sacrament, and its ministers, whether in terms of all its members or of a group of specialists, are ministers only in the same service of word and sacrament. To be a minister apart from the substance and purpose of ministry would clearly, from what we have already seen of the nature of the Church, be a strange sort of ministry.

We come then to the Christian understanding of ministry. We have seen that the purpose of the whole Christian community is *diaconia*, service, and in this sense there is a *diaconia* or priesthood of all believers. This service is entirely dependent on Christ, and on his continuing ministry through the Holy Spirit. Any sort of ministry has its authority only in the ministry of Christ.

There has long been in Christian communities a group of people set aside to look after the community, until recently usually in a full-time capacity. Gradually they came to be of increasing importance, as hierarchical structures of institutional ministry grew. The purpose of these people has been differently understood at different times. Their image has not always been good. By contrast with the high standards theoretically required of a ministry of God's word, their conduct has often inevitably seemed inadequate, and has sometimes been abominable. Chaucer's question has often been relevant: 'If gold rust, what shall iron do?' But sometimes too the Christian ministry has been the salt of the earth. There is here a record of self-effacing service as the instruments of God's love, faithful to the point of death in concentration camps and similar places, which must be unmatched in human history.

DOCTRINAL DEVELOPMENTS

What does the biblical background to the doctrine of the ministry look like?

In the Old Testament period there were numerous special offices in Israel. People had responsibility for various aspects of social life. There were leaders of tribes, of clans, in the synagogue. The military leaders of Israel were often thought to have charismatic quality. Seers, prophets and priests had special charismatic authority. Priests, in making sacrifice, looking after oracles and giving religious advice, had a special power which came to their office. The same came to be true of the king, as the son and the servant of God.

The growth of Christian communities in New Testament times produced various organisational problems. These were dealt with by the allotment of different sorts of duties to different people. The central task was the preaching of the coming kingdom, the proclamation of the resurrection as the inauguration of the kindgom, and the communal life of the people awaiting this imminent occurrence. Clearly this programme did not envisage a developmental period of at least two thousand years. The main authority is that of 'the twelve', which is understood to go back to Jesus. Further developments arose after the pattern of analogous Jewish religious groups, though not, as in Qumran, as an exclusive parallel cult awaiting the end in an atmosphere of strict discipline. Well-defined offices in the later sense simply did not exist in this period, as von Campenhausen has demonstrated.[1] The apostle has authority in the whole Church, and the elders in the local community. The relationships between the universal and the local communities had yet to be spelled out.

St Paul understood his apostolic authority not as an inherent special quality but as based on his calling by the Lord to his service. Power and authority in the Church are for him the power of the Spirit. The service of the Church is performed through the activity of the Spirit, whether this takes place through apostles, prophets or teachers. When a hierarchical order of the church arises, as reflected in the pastoral letters and in Ignatius, it does so as a consequence of the need to set up a permanent social institution and to guard against heresy. In this process the growth of concepts of apostolic succession play a basic role. Soon the communities begin to think of orderly succession without dissension, and of the process of handing over spiritual authority.

The history of the understanding of ministry is in large part the development of the various images and pressures which are represented in the diversity of the biblical narratives themselves. The main turning points are in the same thinkers whom we considered in looking at the history of the Church. *Origen* and *Cyprian* both see the basis of the Church's office in the bishop. In place of Christ the bishop offers forgiveness of sins. Stress is laid in the East on the spiritual and charismatic aspects of this power, and in the West on its more juridical consequences. In the West the primacy of the bishop of Rome came increasingly to be maintained, whereas in the East a collegiate understanding of the episcopate was retained.

At the time of the Reformation the forgiveness of sins was tied more closely again to the preaching of the word rather than to the possession of high spiritual office. In traditional Roman Catholic understanding of priesthood there were to be two interrelated hierarchies, of consecration and jurisdiction. Consecration qualified for office, which then regulates the manner of further consecration, and of the administration of the sacraments. The Pope is bishop for all and has full sacramental and juridical authority over all the faithful. The Orthodox Churches have a similar understanding of hierarchy, but without the papal primacy. As far as church jurisdiction is concerned, the laity has a much larger role. Reformed Churches have traditionally stressed alongside the ministers of the word the roles of deacons, elders and teachers in the instruction and discipline of congregations. Lutherans have laid more exclusive stress on preaching as the central office in the congregation. Other groups, e.g. Quakers, have abandoned the whole idea of ordained ministers set aside from other Christians as fundamentally misleading in a Christian community.

CONTEMPORARY MODELS

What then are we to make of the Christian understanding of the ministry in the face of all these various possibilities and combinations? It is worthwhile looking here at the comments of our earlier guides.

Moltmann begins from the position that the whole Christian ministry has prophetic, priestly and messianic service to fulfill. Community and particular assignments are dependent on one another. 'For a long time people in the Church thought in a quite one-sided way from Christ to the office, and from the office to the Christian fellowship.'[2] As he sees it, the growth in the early Church of the monarchial episcopate broke up the relationship between the commissioned Church and its many special commissions in a way that was totally one-sided.

As assignments for the Church in the world vary, so forms of ministry are historically variable. 'Their number and form can be fixed neither through the myth of a transfigured past, nor through the ideal of a utopian future.' There remain certain essential functions of the messianic liberation of the world. These are (1) the charge to proclaim the gospel, (2) the charge to baptise and to celebrate the Lord's Supper, (3) the charge to lead the community's assemblies, and (4) the charge to carry out charitable work. These are *kerygma*, *koinonia* and *diaconia*. Central is the conviction that traditional prejudices must not be allowed to quench the Spirit and hinder the charismatic powers from their service for the kingdom.

The service of the community is not only local but universal and ecumenical. The universality of the Church can be expressed through a representative office of unity. The community needs wider ecumenical and conciliar ministries. It will discover the charismata for them and will bestow the appropriate commissions. Such commissions should be neither archaically romantic nor fashionably pragmatic, but should represent openness to the Spirit in the future.

The commission of the Church is based on the service of the disciples and so is apostolic. Apostolic succession points not only backwards but forwards, conveys the unique nature of the messianic community as a whole, and is therefore not to be narrowed down to one office, e.g. the episcopate. There is much more than we can explore here in Moltmann's study, dealing with traditions, successions and historical continuity, the Church as fellowship, Church and state and other related issues.

Küng begins his discussion of ministry in a remarkably similar way to Moltmann. First comes the priesthood of all believers, a priesthood entirely and completely dependent on Christ as the only high priest and mediator. In striking contrast to the high emphasis placed on Mariology by Pope John Paul II, it is interesting to note that in the five hundred pages of Küng's text there appears to be no mention of Mary at all. Once again, as in Protestant writings, there appear to be almost as many Catholic theologies as there are theologians.

Christ is the fulfilment and the end of a special priestly caste. 'The abolition of a special priestly caste and its replacement by the priesthood of the one new and eternal high priest has as its strange yet logical consequence the fact that all believers share in a universal priesthood.'[3] The reality of this priesthood is that all are called to preach the gospel in their personal Christian witness, without all being called in the narrow sense of the word, or called to be theologians. Every Christian is empowered to take an active part in baptism, eucharist and the forgiveness of sins. All live before God for others and are supported by others.

Christian service is the service of Christ. As in the New Testament, special ministries are there for the community, and can be exercised in a variety of different forms. The apostolic succession of pastoral ministry is part of the apostolic succession of the community. What then of Petrine power and ministry? The historical claims of Petrine succession are hard to justify. Each branch of the Church has its own tradition, and these may continue for the welfare of all, if properly understood. Any Petrine primacy must be a primacy of service, a pastoral primacy.

In 1936 Ramsey saw a traditional understanding of historic apostolic succession of the sort found in the Anglican Church as a direct consequence of the gospel. Properly understood, the episcopate is the *esse* of the universal Church. As for Church order, the outward order of the Church is of supreme importance. 'The structure of Catholicism is an utterance of the gospel.' But even here the structure is not the essence, and Ramsey later suggested that preoccupation with structure was not his last word on the subject. In writing on the Holy Spirit he said that it is a mistake in ecclesiology to dwell exclusively on one of the images of the Church and to press its implications with a rigorous kind of logic.[4]

GUIDELINES

In considering some of the basic elements of ministry we find then at least the following features. The gospel is given to the Christian community, not indeed as a possession but as something to be shared with others. It is given through the Holy Spirit, through the preaching of the word and the sharing of the sacraments. It comes through communication in word and action in Church and wider community. All Christians are hearers and doers of the word, and in that sense all are equally endowed with a spiritual character, in so far as they remain faithful servants. Some are set apart in the community to preach and administer the sacraments. This gives them no more spiritual character. But it does give them a particular spiritual office within the congregation. Those who take up such office are called by God through the community to do so. Their ministry, like all Christian life, is human response. But it is response to the service of God who is its end and fulfilment.

It goes without saying that the various Christian understandings of ministry have become hallowed with ancient cultural connotations. These have good and bad connotations for ecumenical development. Bishops for example, as Michael Ramsey has pointed out, have for centuries in Scotland been regarded, for good historical reasons, as epitomising a superior, arrogant sort of English imperialist overlord. Scottish presbyteries, as Ramsey was kind enough not to point out, have often for equally good reasons been regarded (notably by the national bard) as a byword for bigotry, hypocrisy and cant. Yet there have been both saintly bishops and enlightened presbyteries, whose influence has been directed for good in Church and society. Here we may have to bring in the new world to redress the balance of the good, if we are not to remain prisoners of the bitterness born of past inhumanity, as in the tragedy of Northern Ireland.

In this context it is fashionable to look for new functional definitions and concepts of ministry. But unless theologically satisfactory concepts are produced, socially and pastorally orientated frameworks will not do the whole job. In such a process both the intellectual freedoms won at considerable cost in the European intellectual tradition and the social and cultural freedoms won in the Churches of the so-called third world may be of value. The theological foundations we shall consider further in the second part of this study.

7 Christ, word and sacrament

THE SACRAMENTAL TRADITION

The centre of the gospel is Jesus Christ, and he is made known in Christian community through word and sacrament. In this section we shall consider what is meant by 'sacrament'. For some branches of the Church sacraments are the heart of the gospel. For others they are at best peripheral and at worst positively misleading. Here, perhaps even more than elsewhere, the divergences go straight back to central features of the biblical narratives themselves.

In the New Testament we find no single term corresponding to the traditional use of 'sacrament'. There is no single term which covers both baptism and the Lord's supper, not to speak of the five other sacraments of the medieval Church. The Greek equivalent of the Latin *sacramentum* is *mysterion*. Mysterion described the secret cultic ritual in the Greek mystery religions and in Gnosticism. It appears too in the Septuagint and in apocalyptic writings. In the New Testament it refers to the mystery of the divine Lordship (Mark 4:11f.) and in Paul to the *kerygma*, the preaching of the word (1 Cor. 2:1,2:7, etc). In Colossians Christ is the *mysterion* of God (2:2 cf. 2:7;4:3). The *mysterion* is the hidden wisdom of God, which is disclosed in the revelation in Christ. There are other references to for example the final destiny of Israel, or marriage, as *mysterion*.

Justin Martyr was the first to bring together baptism and the eucharist as the same sort of mystery. The connection of *mysterion* as a sacred rite with baptism and communion was made by *Tertullian* and *Cyprian*. They use the Latin *sacramentum* as equivalent to *mysterion* in the sense of initiation into the sacred rite, in language in some ways closer to that of the Greek religions than that of the New Testament use of *mysterion*. Tertullian sees the sacrament as the given place of the revelation of salvation, where God has bound himself and men to meet. Other actions, like chrism and ordination, were added. Gradually there emerges the idea of a sacrament as an external act ordained by God, through which the recipients participate in a special way in God's blessings. All of this haphazard coming together is rather different from the crisp uncomplicated picture of the New Testament institution of the sacraments by Jesus which we unfold in our service books. Liturgy is not historical monograph.

Critical influence on the concept of a sacrament was exercised by *Augustine*, who always thought of sacrament as a term including baptism and eucharist. Augustine distinguished between the sign (*signum*) and the thing signified (*res*), between the action with the elements and the inner working of divine grace. The two aspects were linked through the word of institution and consecration. The eucharist is effective only if the word of promise is believed. The sacraments have a significative and spiritual meaning, and also a realistic and effective meaning. Later both these sides were to be developed in different ways and with varying emphasis.

In the West in the middle ages the effective character of the sacraments was emphasised. Stress was laid on the presence in essence of the spiritual powers in the consecrated elements (*Paschasius*). A more spiritual interpretation was followed by *Ratramnus*, and by *Berengar of Tours*, who was made by his opponents to recant and to confess that in the eucharist the believer drinks the actual blood and crunches with his teeth the body of Christ. The spiritual line of interpretation was to be developed further in medieval times especially by *Bonaventure* and *Duns Scotus*. We find now too a much wider range of opinion than before. Groups like the Cathars, in opposition to the central authority of Rome, placed little emphasis on sacraments. On the other hand, all forms of blessing in the Church came to be regarded as sacramental. The favourite medieval picture was of seven sacraments, but sometimes there were thought to be five, nine, twelve or even thirty, some of more importance than others.

The great sacramental theologians of the middle ages were *Hugo of St Victor* and then *Thomas Aquinas*. Thomas added to the Augustinian sign and things signified the further divisions of form and matter. Spiritual power lies in the sacraments themselves, and they represent and transmit this power. Sacraments are necessary for salvation, and their effectiveness depends not on the moral purity of the celebrant but on his intention, to do what Christ and the Church commanded. In Thomas and his successors all is still a matter of exploration and discussion. At the Council of Trent a definitive statement of the nature of sacraments was produced. There are seven sacraments, all instituted by Christ. Form and material are defined. They have effective character. That is to say, they contain and transmit grace. They are necessary for salvation, and work *ex opere operato*, of their own accord. A sacramental character of an indelible sort is conferred through baptism, confirmation and priestly ordination. Here the mysteries of the gospel are parcelled into tidy definitions.

The Orthodox Church, partly under the influence of western Catholicism, developed a sacramental teaching with seven sacraments, but without the rigid legal and conceptual uniformity characteristic of Tridentine thought. As we shall see, in any case the definitions of Trent have not prevented a remarkable further discussion in Catholic thought, and this has borne fruit especially in this century.

At the Reformation, in some areas of doctrine there were fewer changes than might perhaps have been expected. But in the teaching on the sacraments there were major developments. The Reformers denied the validity of seven sacraments and allowed only two. Baptism and the Lord's Supper alone were held to have been instituted by Christ. The sacraments are based on the word of God, and lead to salvation only when they are received in faith. The main means of grace is the preached word. On the relation of word and sacrament there are differing opinions. *Luther* and the Lutheran tradition stressed the effective character of the sacraments. God's Word takes the elements into its power and brings to man the reality of that which the words of institution promise. Sacraments strengthen faith and are vehicles of the word of salvation.

Other Reformers viewed the matter rather differently. It is never wise to imagine that 'the Reformers' all thought alike. After all, they were real people in different sorts of circumstances, not embodied reflections of leather bound volumes all in the same series! *Zwingli* characteristically rejected the word 'sacrament' as unbiblical. For him baptism and the Lord's Supper are basically symbolic actions. They are a reminder in physical form to the Christian of the salvation which Christ has brought to him. They are also means through which Christians in community confess their faith in Christ before each other and the world. Basically they neither produce nor strengthen faith. The subject of the action is not Christ but the faithful Christian congregation.

Calvin produced his own teaching, which was to be, not indeed a pale compromise between Lutheran and Zwinglian positions but a new approach which would, among other things, have the best of both concepts. Against Zwingli, Calvin stressed that God is the subject of the sacramental actions. These are instituted by God to seal and strengthen his word of salvation and our faith. Only then are they to be seen as an instrument of Christian witness in the world. Against the Lutheran scheme Calvin understood the preached word as the main instrument of the transmission of the gospel, to which the sacraments are added as a 'sign and seal'. The sacraments are not identical with the power of the Holy Spirit, but receive their power from the Spirit. There is a parallel rather than an identity between the work of the Spirit and the sacraments. The sacraments are effective only for those who believe. For others they are empty signs. For believers they have effective character.

In all this discussion it is important to remember that for a very large number of Christians sacraments have traditionally been regarded as essentially peripheral to the gospel. This is particularly the case in many Baptist and Congregationalist Independent traditions, and indeed in many others. Because writers on sacramental topics generally come from traditions in which the sacraments are regarded highly, we must consciously bear in mind that many millions of Christians have lived and died without any explicit consciousness of sacramental piety. For them faith in community is sustained by the word as sacrament. In such traditions baptism may be understood as acceptance into the community in a wider sense, and the Lord's Supper as an expression of the reality of the Christian community as community.

Much of the reinterpretation of sacraments which has taken place has been influenced by developments in European thought since the Enlightenment. In the more traditional denominations, the liturgy and the sacraments are perhaps the last areas of doctrine to be so affected. So for example we find in some distinctively modernist theologians in the Anglican communion a deep reverence for traditional sacramental piety. But it was characteristic of the Enlightenment that it regarded sacraments as pious usages with symbolic meaning, to be used for strengthening the moral purpose of the community. *Schleiermacher*, who preferred to speak of 'mysteries' rather than sacraments, did not want to abolish them but to see them as 'activities of Christ through which he sustains and develops the relationship between himself and us'. In this direction as in many others Schleiermacher has been the father of modern Protestant theology.[1] Here too his influence on Karl Barth may be noticed.

THE TWENTIETH CENTURY

Having seen something of the development in history it is worth turning back to our selection of distinguished modern 'theological guinea pigs' to see what they come up with on sacraments. Michael Ramsey moves from discussion of worship and liturgy immediately to the eucharist. The eucharist, like all Christian prayer, is to be interpreted in the light of the whole of the New Testament. Its meaning cannot be exhausted in the context of the Last Supper, for in it Jesus declares the whole meaning of (1) redemption and (2) creation. An understanding of the eucharist as a mirror of incarnation and covenant is not uncommon among theologians who find no historical evidence that the Last Supper actually took place, but want to retain eucharistic theology. However, we can probably assume that such was not Ramsey's motive in 1936.

With its series of elements of thanksgiving, commemoration, mystery, fellowship and sacrifice, the eucharistic liturgy declares the whole meaning of the gospel and of the one body. The liturgy is the summing up of the New Testament, and a key to the meaning of all life. Typically, thirty years later he could criticise the over-use of the image of the church as the body. This ability to develop, neither constantly shifting position nor dying in the last ditch for one's early dogmatic pronouncements, is an impressive aspect of Ramsey's work – well worth blatant imitation![2]

Küng also considers the sacraments in the context of the Body of Christ. He begins with baptism. Baptism itself is of no value. Baptism and *metamoia*, baptism and faith, go together. Faith and baptism do not have their bases in themselves, but alike in the saving act of God in Christ. By the sign of water the word of grace which is effective in a man is confirmed. Baptism gives man such a radically new character that he can receive it only once.

Küng now looks at the theology of the Lord's Supper. The Lord's Supper in the New Testament reflects recollection and thanksgiving for the past, presence in the present, and hope for the future. 'The *word* is decisive in the Lord's Supper as in baptism. The elements by themselves have no significance, and it is in the light of the word that we should understand the Lord's Supper.'[3] The bread and the wine are signs, but effective signs, containing what they represent. The Lord's Supper is fellowship with Christ, and so fellowship with other Christians.

Moltmann's account of the sacramental tradition is very similar to that of Küng. He lays particular stress on the eucharist as a sign of God's dealings with the world, and as an open feast: 'Anyone who celebrates the Lord's supper in a world of hunger and oppression does so in complete solidarity with the sufferings and hopes of all men, because he believes that the Messiah invites all men to his table and because he hopes that they will all sit at table with him.'[4]

TOWARDS A THEOLOGY OF THE SACRAMENTS

Something should be said here about the vexed question of infant baptism. Moltmann offers some suggestions for a new baptismal practice. The way to a new, more authentic baptismal practice will be the way from infant to adult baptism. A service of blessing in infancy would be followed by baptism later. Baptism would however be based, as always, not on the individual's motivation but on God's grace. He argues that so-called voluntary baptism does not really make baptism a matter of choice. For it is essentially baptism into the liberty of Christ.

In this emphasis Moltmann is following Karl Barth, in his controversial advocacy of adult rather than infant baptism in his *Church Dogmatics* IV 4. Barth sees water baptism as above all the authentically human response to God's baptism of men through the Holy Spirit in Jesus Christ.

The authentically human response may of course be at the same time the work of the Holy Spirit. As Barth himself says in the same volume, 'There is no more intimate friend of an authentically human understanding of man than the Holy Spirit.' It may then be possible in principle for both infant and adult baptism to be seen as equally part of the eschatological dimension of God's spiritual calling and man's freely given response. An argument along similar lines may be found in Geoffrey Lampe's study *The Seal of the Spirit*.[5] It is perhaps worth mentioning that there is a considerable polemical literature on Barth's treatment of baptism. Much of this appears to me to be more clever than sound.

I return here to the underlying issue: What is a sacrament? We saw that both Calvin and Luther followed the Augustinian distinction of sign and thing signified. Sacraments were means of grace instituted and commanded by Christ for the strengthening of the Christian community. More precisely they were instruments of the word of God. For the Reformed tradition in particular, the audible word in preaching was in some respects prior to the visible word in the sacraments. The Holy Spirit possesses a sovereign freedom which is not tied by any necessity to the sacramental action. The Spirit's presence is a presence of grace alone. Still, Calvin would probably have agreed with Luther's complaint, against undue spiritualising, that everything that is claimed to come from the Spirit, apart from the Word and Sacrament, is of the devil.

But the word, it may be reflected, is the word of God, Father, Son and Spirit. Luther came to reflect, and this has been taken up by *Barth, Eberhard Jüngel, Edward Schillebeeckx* and others, that Christ is the primary and indeed the sole sacrament of God for the world. The other 'sacraments' are strictly speaking sacramental signs deriving from God's engagement in his creation through Jesus Christ. Spelling this out further, we may say that incarnation and atonement are outward and visible signs of God's hidden spiritual presence in creation. The sacraments are effective signals of the nature of God as self-giving love at work in the created universe.

We may end this section by thinking again of the question of the presence of Christ, and the long battles about the nature of the presence. A Christianity based on past and future without present is at best a rather poor affair, anything but the good news of the gospel. Christ is present to his people in word and sacrament. His sacramental presence is known only to faith. But this does not make his presence either subjective or exclusive. It is Christ, and not our imagination, that is the promise of the gospel, though our imagination may be used in the service of faith's apprehension. It is Christ the Lord of creation who is present in his Church. Somewhat as in human communities, relationship within one community need not inhibit equally full relationship within other, overlapping communities. So the sacrifice of Christ in the past is made present as real presence in the present.

In his excellent study of eucharistic worship and theology my colleague Nicholas Lash put it like this:

> The sacrifice of Christ will continue to be present in history through its effective commemoration, which commemoration, as effective, draws from the men to whom God in Christ is thus made present in the spirit the praise of faithful love and service. . . . To say that the real presence of Christ in the consecrated bread and wine is a presence to faith is not to say that it is a 'merely spiritual' presence, whatever that would mean. People only become present to each other, communicate with each other, through a bodily sharing.[6]

Christians, who believe in God as creator, see the triune God as the most intimate presence in all creation, and see in the presence of Christ in the Lord's Supper a particular realisation of the new creation in a presence continuous with the creative presence of God through the Holy Spirit, the spirit of the risen Christ.

PART II

THE CHURCH OF THE LOVE OF GOD

8 Structuring elements of doctrine: the Church

THE CHURCH OF THE SPIRIT

The Christian faith is about God, for whom to be is to love, and about God's love for all mankind. The nature of God as love was demonstrated uniquely and decisively in human history in the events concerning Jesus Christ. God continues this relationship through the work of the Spirit in the world. He continues to love, expressing his love in concern for the welfare, the unity and the reconciliation with himself and each other of all human beings. It is then only, but also precisely as a central instrument of the gospel of God's love, that the Church plays its part in the future of God's new creation. The Church is the Church of the love of God or else it is nothing. It is there for all, as Jesus Christ lived and died and was resurrected for the salvation of all mankind. The ground of the Church's existence and action in the love of God should then be the basis of all theory and practice in ecclesiology. It is rarely possible to produce simple correspondences between ultimate foundation and practical outworking. Unless this basis in the love of God in Jesus Christ informs the whole structure, little progress can be expected. 'Apart from me you can do nothing.' Of course, horrendous crimes have been committed in the name of the love of God, but unless this basis is constantly recollected, after the pattern of the gospel, little can be done.

Christians believe, however differently this belief is expressed, that human beings, men, women and children, are created by God and are given a special place of privilege and responsibility within the created order. Such a common heritage is dependent on neither race nor creed, intellectual and physical capacity or incapacity. They grow up, socially and individually, in a culture in which they are partially responsive, partly unresponsive, to the implications of the divine love. They may become more aware of the reconciling love of God through the communication of the message of salvation in Christ, the word incarnate. But the Christian communities soon became aware that the receiving of the message of divine reconciliation was not exactly like the receiving of a message of any other sort. However variously we may interpret the historical events, this awareness was an awareness of something unusual, reflected *par excellence* in the experience of the Spirit at Pentecost, and reflected too in references throughout the New Testament to the Spirit, the Spirit of Christ, the Holy Spirit.

The receiving of the gospel and the conduct of life in devotion to God and man was and is understood by the Christian communities not as the result of moral or intellectual effort, but as a gift of God. The fellowship of the Holy Spirit is the medium of the grace of the Lord Jesus Christ, through which we are sustained in and through the love of God. So long as we remember this intimate connection between the Spirit and Christ, reflecting the love of God for all his creation, then we can say that it is particularly in the perspective of the doctrine of the Holy Spirit that we may understand the life of the Christian in community.

THE CHRISTIAN COMMUNITY

How then are we to specify the structuring elements of the Christian community, the Church? This has been done, and may be done, in innumerable different ways. In the sixteenth article of the Scots Confession of 1560 the Church is described as 'a company and multitude of men chosen by God, who rightly worship and embrace him by true faith in Jesus Christ, who is the only head of the same Kirk.'[1] The confession then goes on to speak of the notes of the true Kirk of God, which are the true preaching of the word, the right administration of the sacraments and, last and typically Reformed, 'ecclesiastical discipline uprightly administered, as God's word prescribes, whereby vice is repressed and virtue nourished'. The true preaching of the word and the right administration of the sacraments are of course the distinctive marks of the Church in a host of Reformation confessions, the most famous expression of which is perhaps article seven of the Lutheran *Confessio Augustana*.

It is a far cry from such definitions to such modern works as J. C. Hoekendijk's excellent *The Church Inside Out*.[2] Yet if it is true that experience of evil in the world is one of the main obstacles to Christian belief today, I think it may also be said that experience of Christian life in community is one of the main ways, indeed *the* main way, paradoxical as it sometimes seems, in which people come to faith. It is much easier to think in abstract about religious and theological problems in general than to think out the concrete implications of Christian life in community. It is even more difficult, in a world in which the complexities of 'real life' often seem to rule out any actualisation of 'life in Christ' in the communion of saints, to turn theory into practice. Yet a theology which stops short of the Christian community in theory and practice is more than inconsequential.

The speculations of churchmen and theologians often seem light years away from the realities, some indescribably trivial and some indescribably all-embracing, of the modern world. It is perfectly proper for scholarship to be pursued in a scholarly atmosphere. But the Church makes, not for herself but for service in God's name, the most comprehensive claims. It follows that a theology of the Church must attempt to offer a contribution to the understanding of community which amounts to more than musty or even freshly printed volumes reflecting the preoccupations of moth-eaten institutions. Theology is not the centre of the Church and theory is no substitute for practice. But practice should be able to count on the maximum assistance from the theoretical side.

THE CHURCH OF JESUS CHRIST

The biblical narratives reflect both the centrality and the diversity of concern for community among early Christians. The focus, fulfilment and transformation of community expectation is the life, death and resurrection of Jesus Christ. We have seen that in the Old Testament one of the main strands of theological reflection is centred on the idea of the people of God. The people of God arises out of God's covenant with Israel at Sinai. This is the people whom God has chosen to make his name known. To this people the law was given. Despite their sins, a remnant of this people will be saved by God in the day when a new covenant will be made. In the New Testament, Jesus comes through the gospel narratives as one who searches for the people of God, a people to be gathered round his own person in waiting for the coming of the kingdom. Jesus gathers a small group of disciples. His new temple is the community of those who believe in him as God's agent in bringing in the kingdom (Matt. 13:2; 14:58). The task of those who believe is to spread the message of the kingdom. In Acts the Church is the people of God, for whom the promises of the New Testament are realised in Christ (2:25f., 38f.). St Paul speaks not only of the Church but of the churches in different places. The Church of God, he says, forms a body (1 Cor. 12:11f.; Rom. 12:5f.) whose head is Christ and whose members are the faithful (1 Cor. 10:16f.; cf. Col. 1:22f.; Eph. 1:22f.). St John speaks not of the Church but of the shepherd and his flock. The Johannine Christ prays that all who believe may be one (17:1ff.) and the relationship is illustrated by the unity of the vine (15:1f.).

The Church in the New Testament is the bride of Christ. It is the building of which Christ is the chief cornerstone. Its members are called. They believe, they are baptised, they continue in faith through worship. They proclaim the gospel of salvation to those outside in word and deed. They may stress different, even contradictory aspects of this nature and task at different times and in different places, but they have these common characteristics.

A Church which is divorced from concern with Christ is clearly, by New Testament standards, an odd sort of Church. But at the same time the doctrine of the Church must not be confused with the doctrine of Christ. The Church is not an extension of the incarnation.

The Church in the New Testament is spoken of as the body of Christ. But it is also referred to as the temple of the Holy Ghost, the Church of God, the people of God. It is founded by the death and resurrection of Christ, but also by the pouring out of the Spirit at Pentecost, the election of the covenant people in the Old Testament, the creation of mankind itself. It is the Church of Father, Son and Spirit. In relation to Christ it is the body only in so far as it is obedient. It is always dependent on Christ. The Church in the New Testament, then, is dependent on faithfulness to Christ. The history of the Church, which we traced in Part I, is the history of the working of the Holy Spirit through Christian failure and discipleship.

We may then say something like this about the relationship between Christ and the Church.

The Church is the people of God, at the same time called into the world and called out of the world by Christ. The Church is called out of the world. Jesus died on the cross for the whole world. Those who follow Christ, the way of the cross, must die to the world and find a new life in Christ. It is often said how easy it is for Christians to be 'other worldly' and to fail to take seriously the claims and duties of this world. This is still true for many groups. But in a secular world, there is also the problem of how to avoid being overwhelmed by the values, concepts, claims and duties of this world. Christians are called out of this world by Christ. But the Church is also the people of God sent out into this world by Christ. Both movements, out of and into the world, belong to the Christian understanding of the Church. The people of God are given the task of communicating in word and action the message of the Lordship of Christ in the world now.

The Church is a worshipping community, in which Christ is present and active. In worship the Church waits on God, who makes himself present to it in word and sacrament. It is through the presence of Christ that the congregation becomes part of the body of Christ. Waiting for God also involves remembrance of God's presence, read of in the Scriptures. It involves thanksgiving in praise and prayer, in confession and petition, in intercession for others, within and outside the Church. This waiting has both a short term and a long term object. The Church waits for Christ, who is experienced as presence in worship now, but who will be seen and known more fully at the end of time. Worshipping and waiting, the Church participates in the new creation yet to come, though she is not yet that new creation.

As an anticipation of the new creation, the members of the Church may become the medium of the love of Christ to all men, if they are willing to be used in this way. This is the ministry, or natural way of life, of all Christian people, of which we have spoken and which we shall come to consider again.

Within this ministry of the people of God, based on Christ's ministry to men, technical skills and functions may be exercised by any who are trained and qualified for the purpose. Here is the place of the ordained ministry, set apart, and professionals in that they are trained for a particular job. We shall look again at the ministry. The order, as I have put it here, is (1) the ministry of Christ, (2) the ministry of the people of God and (3) the ordained ministry of the gospel. In the tradition of the Church, 2 and 3 are often reversed. In my understanding of the matter, the structure of the professional ministry, whole or part time, will depend largely on the nature of the situation in which it is to work.

ONE, HOLY, CATHOLIC AND APOSTOLIC

The Church, according to the Nicene creed, 'is one, holy, catholic and apostolic'. These are eschatological pointers, to which its particular manifestations rarely correspond completely, but they remain important in pointing to God's purpose for his Church.

As the one Church in Christ, the Church is called to be a unity: 'that they all may be one'. Already in the New Testament there are all sorts of squabbling factions and congregations with widely differing views. There will no doubt always be differences in Christian theory and practice, as in all other areas of society, and uniformity is to be avoided. But in central affirmations and in discipleship there ought to be unity. The disunited is the abnormal, the united the normal state of affairs. Peace is the appropriate, war the inappropriate state of affairs. To unite with other Christian bodies is not of course just to swallow them up: we shall come to speak of practical ecumenism again. The Church is one.

The Church is holy. The holiness of the Church is in the first place not the holiness, the transparent goodness and love of its members, but the holiness of Christ. If the members fail to profit from the invitation of Christ, then they are members in name only. The Church is catholic. It encompasses the whole of this planet. Its concern is as much with the children of the refugee camps as with the choristers of Canterbury or the citizens of Chicago. The Church is apostolic. It is only as the bearer of the witness of the time of the events concerning Jesus that the Church can communicate a distinctive message to mankind.

We shall return to these attributes. We may notice, too, that the Church is often said to be indestructible. The gospel is not an offer available for a limited period only. The promise of God is there as long as there are human beings alive, and it continues beyond physical death. God promises always to be with his people, however difficult conditions may become. A corollary of this is that the Church is visible in the world. There was in the tradition, and still is, room for concepts of the invisible Church. Only God can say who is 'in Christ' and who only appears to be, but in fact rejects God's love. On the other hand, there is no need to allow such concepts as 'by faith alone' and 'the hiddenness of revelation' to take away reality from the concrete existence of a Christian community of discipleship. The Church then is visible. But though visible it may also be, in whole or in part, unfaithful. The actions of the Church or part of it are always subject to the judgement of God. The visible community can never simply equate its will with God's will.

Finally, the promise of the divine perfection and consummation of creation is also the hope of the Church. The perfection of creation is the fulfilment of the role of the Church, though the Church cannot bring this about alone. In any case, between the times we must be cautious about congratulating ourselves on our understanding of the Church's role, for our practice leaves so much still to be desired. I want to end this section not on the customary note of doxological exaltation but with a reminder of the less positive aspects of the current state of play, from *The Church Inside Out*.

The Christian community therefore is (or should be) an open community, open to everyone who has become a partaker in the same *shalom*. In practice this is not the case. In an unconscious way the national churches have become closed, because they related Christian community and nationality too exclusively, and in the West the Churches have become class churches, because they identified themselves too uncritically with one special group in society. It is nonsense to call these churches to evangelism, if we do not call them simultaneously to a radical revision of their life and a revolutionary change in their structure.[3]

9 Structuring elements of doctrine: ministry

AUTHORITY AND POWER

The search for structuring elements of the doctrine of the ministry brings a number of new considerations sharply into play. Here we are concerned not only with issues of theological structure and spiritual authority, but also with matters of power and privilege, in the nature of leadership and control, exercised by individuals or by groups. Perhaps nowhere does the ambivalent nature of the Church come to the fore more than in discussion of such issues.

Some of the most perceptive writing on this problem of the relation between spiritual authority and temporal power has come from America. Paul Tillich in volume three of his *Systematic Theology* wrote eloquently of the gap between the Church and the Kingdom of God, and of the demonisation which occurs when the Church confuses aspirations to spiritual and to temporal power.[1] H. R. Niebuhr pointed to the evils inherent in much of the ruthless grasping for and retention of privileges of all kinds inherent in denominationalism.[2] On the other side of the Atlantic, Ian Henderson has written, with the unfair but searching penetration of the one-sided observation, of Anglican imperialism and its use of doctrines of apostolic succession against American and Scottish churches: 'The docrine of apostolic succession enables Englishmen to give expression to institutional narcissism in the ecclesiastical orb just as the romanticism of Oxford and Cambridge has enabled them to do so in the academic one.'[3]

Of course it is equally true that Americans and Scots have had their own ways of returning such tactics in similar style. But the quotation illustrates the severity of the difficulties. I have commented that concern with church structures in ecumenical theology may be an easy way of opting out from facing the problems of the real world. But it might also be thought that much recent 'ecumenical' concern with ecology, science, liberation and anything but church structures is an equally dubious escape from ecumenical reality. It may be based on the tacit admission that none of the major denominations is prepared, for the foreseeable future, to give up anything at all of its entrenched theories and privileges, especially regarding the nature of ministerial authority and ministerial power.

We must never lose sight of the harsh reality of the problems and attractions of power and privilege. All of us like power and privilege. None of us uses them wisely all the time. This is a root problem. Henderson constantly emphasised that there is nothing like the possibility of becoming a bishop, with concomitant powers and privileges to taste in different cultures, to turn the senior ecumenical mind, in the old world, the new world, the third world. The exceptions, we may suspect, prove the rule. This does not of course rule out episcopacy – all forms of authority have their own temptations – but it pinpoints a problem. Comprehensive sociological analyses of the nature and distribution of authority in various ministerial structures may be found in such studies as Mady A. Thung's *Precarious Organisation*.[4] But I want to concentrate here on the theological issues.

EXCLUSIVE POWER

It will be seen on reflection that there is nothing in the comments of our selected theologians, Moltmann, Küng and Ramsey, which precludes in principle the development of a doctrine of the ministry to which all of them could subscribe. Even Ramsey's earlier notion of historical episcopal succession is later modified in such a way, with the aid of christological reflection, that it could be acceptable to Moltmann's Reformed ecclesiology. In such a model for ecumenical action, doctrinal differences would not be sufficient to split the churches. The problem area would be the practical factors of executive authority. This is often the case in ecumenical negotiations.[5]

It would be unwise to think that the theological differences between the churches are thereby eliminated. It seems certain that there will always be those, usually Protestants, who believe that there is *a* biblical doctrine of the ministry, which must be reflected accurately today and which precludes the adoption of institutions like episcopacy, at least as it has been in the history of the Church. There will always be those Roman Catholics, but not indeed all Roman Catholics, who believe in a historically transmitted apostolic succession of supreme power from Christ to his successors in the See of Rome, power only now being properly understood in its full dimensions since the declaration of papal infallibility at Vatican I, power emanating as much from Mary the Mother of God as from Christ her Son. There will always be others, among Anglicans, Lutherans and Calvinists, who believe that the historical form of their own ministerial structures is that exclusively authorised and validated by the Holy Spirit.

The inveterate tendency of theological committees to ascribe their aspirations of the moment to the prompting of the Holy Spirit is of course trying until one has got used to the technique. Again Henderson is devastating:

> The motives which the Anglicans and their fellow-travellers ascribe to themselves in Ecumenical literature are of the highest, being devotion to the Will of God or the Holy Spirit. Up till now this intriguing lack of modesty has paid off. It is only recently that the public has begun to react to the Ecumenical's unending professions of enthusiasm for the Will of God and the Holy Spirit with faint but unmistakeable signs of nausea.[6]

Of course one might reflect that Calvin's victims in Geneva and the Anabaptists mutilated by good Lutherans in the Thirty Years' War might have thought that there were worse martyrdoms than having to bear with a little Anglican oneupmanship.

ECUMENICAL MINISTRY

The literature of the World Council of Churches illustrates endless schemes of union and discussion of projects for the solution of the problems of ministerial function and authority. In South India, in Canada, Australia and to a limited extent in America, schemes of union involving agreed doctrines of ministry have worked remarkably well. But in the Old World little has moved. Bearing in mind that the Lutheran churches in Germany have still not reached a satisfactory understanding among themselves after at least a hundred and fifty years of negotiations, it would be optimistic in the highest degree to expect rapid progress. On the contrary, dogmatic and intellectually untenable positions flourish as churches more and more turn in upon themselves in panic before the accelerating pace of change. Obscurantism is increasingly in fashion, the more recondite the better.

Before trying to gather together the basic lines of a doctrine of ministry we might take a brief look at a good recent study, Richard Hanson's *Christian Priesthood Examined*.[7] Hanson considers the millions who expect to find *a* scriptural doctrine of the ministry and concludes that 'of official Christian priests we must honestly admit that there is in the New Testament not the faintest whisper.' Looking at Church history he sees the development of an historical understanding of priesthood in historical episcopal succession, as a sacerdotal caste. This, however, is to be rejected as a distortion of true Christian ministry. With the coming of Christ all sacrificing cultic priesthood has become insignificant and emptied of purpose. The true priest acts for men to God and for God to men. For the early Church the bishop was the priest *par excellence* because he was the most central and significant minister in the church. So it is today in the Anglican communion, combining Catholic and Protestant elements and providing a ground for reconciliation. 'This I believe to be the destiny of God's providence for the Anglican communion.'

As a critique of biblical fundamentalism on the one hand and sacerdotal fundamentalism on the other this study is excellent. But there is a sense in which, perhaps, on this theory every person who engages in pastoral ministry to a congregation may regard himself or herself as fulfilling the New Testament conception of the bishop in local community. Despite its forward position as a bridge for reconciliation, it is perhaps a little difficult to imagine the Anglican communion rushing to bestow recognition of episcopal status, with all the little courtesies customarily attached, on every parish priest or pastor within reach.

CONFESSIONAL AUTHORITY

For the foreseeable future we are likely to see continuation of the traditional ministerial structures in the older denominations – Lutheran and Reformed, Catholic, Anglican and Orthodox – and the continuation of more modern structures influenced by such notions as democracy in the Free Churches. Something should be said about the use of a word like democracy here. Those of us who belong to the older traditions tend often to react critically to the introduction of such concepts into discussion of church order, though we would die to prevent their exclusion from politics. Yet though we might wish to say that church order comes in important respects from obedience to God's witness in the New Testament rather than from human institutions, the two are not necessarily incompatible. The love of God means equal regard for all men and women. This does not exclude functional hierarchies, in politics, economics, law and science. Simply to express horror at the thought of the relevance of such notions as democracy in Church can scarcely be a wise reaction.

The Roman Catholic church is likely to remain, despite such men as Küng, Congar and Schillebeeckx, conservative in its doctrine of the Church. It is likely to retain its doctrine of an unique historical transmission of truth through those in communion with the Bishop of Rome, with the Pope as the head of a divinely inspired pyramid of authority, with the infallible pronouncements of the Pope, infrequent as they may be, as the supreme continuation of dominical revelation. It can scarcely be overlooked that the Catholicism which is spreading so rapidly in the Third World, though politically radical, is likely to be for some time intellectually, doctrinally and morally conservative. This mood is in many ways typified by the approach of Pope John Paul II, notably in his stress on Mariology, which has found resonance throughout the world. Against this background modern European Catholicism appears as practically liberal Protestantism. Yet it is to Rahner, Küng, Schillebeeckx and their colleagues that we look for contributions towards the solution of the underlying intellectual problems of church order. Much depends on the development of the heritage of Vatican II.

The Orthodox churches are still somewhat divided among themselves. Over against the Western churches they represent a basically uncritical acceptance of the doctrinal formulations of the early ecumenical councils. Here again individual theologians such as Nikos Nissiotis and Jean Meyendorff have developed all manner of imaginative constructive theologies. But though not rejected, their proposals are not likely to be integrated into official theologies, and so are not likely to lead to basic ecumenical reconciliation in the short term.

Lutheran, Reformed and Anglican communions have made limited progress. Documents of ecumenical consensus indicate that the doctrinal differences on ministry need not in principle divide the Churches. But areas of difference remain, and bureaucratic considerations still prevent great practical advance. Moltmann's study was as we have seen essentially based on Lutheran and Reformed traditions.

The Anglican communion is an interesting case. In theory it ought to provide, with its blend of Protestant and Catholic elements, a half-way house to which others may come. In practice others feel that Anglicans too must move, and that their particular virtues are contained already in other confessions, whether Protestant on the one hand or Catholic on the other. What is offered as a *via media* is rejected as a precious and artificial construct. In his excellent study *The Integrity of Anglicanism*[8] Stephen Sykes has called for a new and systematic approach to an Anglican doctrine of the Church, which will neither be a middle way, nor a unity of opposites, nor simply a celebration of what it is to be English, at home or abroad. He sees the springs of such doctrine in liturgy, Sykes is concerned for the ecumenical dimension of the Church, and is worried by the absence of anything like a distinctively Anglican theology of the church. We may agree that a church must have some confidence in its own tradition before it can engage in dialogue with others in a relaxed and constructive manner. A danger with this approach is that it can lead to a greater preoccupation with confessional narrowness. However, all worthwhile theology has its dangers.

MINISTERIAL STRUCTURES

What then of the structuring elements of the doctrine of the ministry? We shall attempt to indicate, not a blueprint for another ecumenical project, but some essential elements.

Ministry in the Church of the love of God, as I understand this, should be seen primarily as the mutual ministry to each other and to all men and women of all Christians. This ministry is not the ministry of Christ, nor may it be thought of in some exactly analogous way to that ministry. But it is based solely on God's gift through grace of the Spirit of the risen Christ.

This special ministry, involving the dedication of people to be employed, full or part time, to preach the word and administer the sacraments, to conduct pastoral work in congregation and community, to offer leadership and direction, may take different forms in different cultures and denominations. These differences would presumably appropriately continue in a united Church, though none of the traditions would remain exactly as they were.

The basic elements of such special ministry are the ministers at local congregational level. These may be priests and deacons, ministers, elders and deacons, bishops, priests and deacons, or other combinations.

In some denominations, such as Congregationalist Independent traditions, the central unit for administrative, liturgical, financial and other purposes will be the single congregation. In others, such as the Lutheran and Reformed traditions, the central unit will be the presbytery, presided over by a chairman or moderator and including probably an equal number of ministers and elders, or a synod presided over by a superintendent or bishop. In Roman Catholic churches the basic unit may be a presbytery of priests, in Anglican churches a diocese presided over by the bishop.

The advantage of the Presbyterian structure is the democratic system (though not all Presbyterians would enjoy the description!) in which all ministers and elders are, in theory at least, equal. Disadvantages include the possible tyranny of permanent secretaries of innumerable committees, and the endless waste of time as everything is discussed by every committee. The advantages of the Anglican system are comparative ease and efficiency at least in theory of administration, and the possibility at least that the bishop *may* have greater pastoral and intellectual gifts than the committee secretary. The basic disadvantage is the danger of undue influence and authority being wielded, individually or collectively, by unwise and authoritarian bishops.

If you believe, as the Roman Catholic church, the Orthodox church and a large part of the Anglican church does, in the dominical institution of an historical succession of episcopacy as a channel of particular grace, then you must have bishops ordained in historical succession in order to have a true church. Those of us who would agree rather with the Anglican scholar Anthony Hanson that 'It has become clear to the great majority of scholars that the traditional doctrine of the apostolic succession cannot be maintained on grounds of historical evidence',[9] will have different priorities, though we shall want to respect the convictions of those who differ. Bishops need not, in principle, represent an insoluble problem for the Reformed tradition, as examples of Reformed, Lutheran and Methodist bishops show. But whether bishops are *always* an advantage to a church remains quite unclear.

What then is needed, it might be thought, is a sufficiently rich and comprehensive structure of church order to allow each to make his or her own interpretation. This is not easy, as the difficulties in the case of the union proposals for South India showed. The effect of mutual recognition of orders in the South India scheme was to produce a situation in which after a generation all ministers would have been ordained in historical succession. Only then would recognition by the Anglican communion follow. Such a proposal was bound to be resisted. If there is to be genuine reconciliation, there must be genuine self-sacrifice and movement on all sides.

If it is granted that bishops may be acceptable, though not mandatory, suitably understood, then there can be no further objection in principle to senior bishops being accorded due respect as archbishops, metropolitans and the like. The Pope as Bishop of Rome may then be seen as part of a symbolic focus of historical continuity in Christendom. Councils and synods may function along with national synods and assemblies for discussion beyond local level. It is scarcely likely that such recognition would permit a union with the Roman Catholic church in the near future; the reality of a divided Christendom is likely to remain. But at least steps may be taken, and unions on a lesser scale undertaken, as steps in the direction of that unity which is part of the eschatological promise of the Church.

In the nature of the case it is inevitable that discussion of ministry should focus upon the person of the minister and his personal role. But the basis of ministry remains not what we do but what God does. The service of the minister is to seek to become an instrument of God's love in Christ for the world. At the same time, this ministry is not a virtuoso performance but takes place within the mutual ministry of all Christians in and for society.

MINISTRY AND WORSHIP

Ministry is not carried out faithfully and effectively through definitions of church order alone, though these may be necessary. Let us consider a situation in which the best forms of church order and doctrines of ministerial office have been agreed by all the churches. Let us assume consensus on the understanding of Church, ministry and sacraments. Let us assume that each minister and congregation is fully committed to Christian service both in congregation and in society. There remains at least one area which is vital to the wellbeing of the Church. This is the dimension of worship, and within this the task of communicating the gospel through preaching. Even where there is evident commitment to pastoral care in congregation and community it is all too easy for worship, and within this preaching, to be neglected. The result may be that a congregation which has flourished for decades suddenly declines sharply.

In the sphere of worship there is still much to be said for the traditional fourfold division of adoration, confession, thanksgiving and intercession. It is not uncommon to have confession and thanksgiving without adoration. But the worship of God in adoration, reflected in praise and prayer, plays an extremely important part in Christian devotion. There is need of confession, for Christians, separately and together, stand much in need of forgiveness. That there is need of thanksgiving should go without saying. Intercession is an equally important part of the agenda for a Church which is called to the service of others, as we join together in participating in God's concern for his people.

It is desirable that worship should be integrally related to all the other activities of life. But it is equally important that the public worship of God should not become yet another ordinary committee meeting. There is all the difference in the world between discussion of adoration and adoration, discussion of confession and confession, discussion of thanksgiving and thanksgiving, discussion of intercession and intercession. Congregations can be and are often literally bored to death.

The problem recurs with renewed urgency in the sphere of preaching. It is particularly unfortunate when the Christian community comes together for worship, perhaps a little tired from their labours, only to go away from worship a little more tired, having been subjected to an essay in elementary moral philosophy which they could have read more easily in bed in the leader columns of their Sunday papers. It is worse when this happens every Sunday.

71

Part of the wonder of human nature made in God's image is its infinite variety. One of the quickest ways to demoralise and dehumanise people is to reduce them to stereotypes, to make them act in monotonous and predictable ways. At a lighter level, one of the secrets of good food is that it should be balanced and varied. The most splendid banquet, if repeated exactly week after week, would speedily become repulsive, while a diet which is seriously deficient in important areas causes rapid physical decay. Yet sermons tend often to provide at best the same sort of rich variety and at worst the same one-sided thin gruel.

The reasons for deficiency are understandable. The pressures of life in the modern parish may be great, particularly in a faithful ministry in a church extension area. Gone are the days of leisurely sermon preparation while the family servants look after vicarage, wife, children and garden. Sermons have to be prepared quickly. The basic issue here is perhaps theological education. If the basic theological education is comprehensive, penetrating and critical, then the sermons are likely to reflect this catholicity, however hastily prepared. If the theological education is one-sided, reflecting modern or traditional fads or shibboleths, then the sermons are almost bound to continue these trends. Now it is clear that no institution can provide *the* correct theological education. Much depends, too, on how minister and congregation work out the implications of the gospel in their own sphere. But the Church's commitment to the gospel of the love of God must clearly include detailed commitment to the best possible theological education at all levels. Experience indicates that this is not minor detail, but a fundamental requirement for the work of the whole Christian community.

THE MINISTRY OF WOMEN

There is one further issue which ought to be tackled here. This is the ministry of women. In the foregoing pages, when I have spoken of mankind, humanity and men, I have naturally and automatically thought of human beings as persons, male and female alike. It appears to me that men and women should share equally in church, ministry and sacraments, and in all areas of human life.

Clearly the issue is a major one, and we must consider the reasons why this is so. The history of mankind is the history of the subjection of some social groups to a position of inferiority by other social groups. Whether this is done savagely, or in a civilised manner, is largely a matter of culture and taste. The results are usually equally distasteful to those who are aware of being regarded as subordinate.

In the case of women most Christians have probably abandoned conscious espousal of doctrines of inequality. But many rightly continue to regard men and women, as having in some respects different roles in society. This is a sociological factor in arguments for the retention of ministry and priesthood by men. Beyond this, it is sometimes argued of the basis of revelation, whether by appeal to the Bible or the church, that God has intended only men to be ministers of word and sacrament in the church. The authority of revelation makes the case of women priests essentially different from that of female lawyers, monarchs, presidents, prime ministers and the like. Thus churches are protected by unique legislative privilege from the implications of such measures as sex discrimination acts.

It was still possible at the second Council of Orange in 529 to debate the issue whether or not a woman was a fully human being, as a man was. Women have come a long way since then! In many churches today women and men engage equally in the mutual pastoral ministry of all believers. Sometimes women have been restricted to certain roles, beyond the ordinary membership of congregations. They have been allowed to participate in minor orders of various sorts, as deaconesses, church sisters and the like. In the Roman Catholic church the veneration of the Virgin Mary has led to increased awareness for and reverence and respect for the faith of women. Mary is the symbol of the centrality of motherhood in human life. But many women wish of course to be regarded as more than simply mothers, and would not consider this sort of veneration as particularly helpful.

In churches where women are ordained to the ministry on the same terms and on the basis of the same training as men, women regard themselves first as ministers and only secondly as women, in exactly the same way as men do. Considerations of sex and gender are rarely directly involved in pastoral ministry in either instance. Congregations have become used to the idea of female ministers, as with female doctors. Certain areas of work, certain types of hospital chaplaincy, may be performed more readily by women, and to such posts women may sometimes gravitate. As in all other spheres of service, having children and being involved in running a home bring their own demands, and require sharing of roles. This comes as a shock to clergymen still accustomed to the male sanctuary of a study and the ladies retiring after dinner, but has less impact on society in general. It is clear that many hundreds of devoted parish ministries have been carried out all over the world in the fifty years or so since the churches first began the ordination of women.

I want to look now at five areas of objection to the ordination of women to the ministry in those churches which have not yet ordained women.[10]

We begin with the argument from the doctrine of scripture. In the biblical narratives women share the subordinate role that was customary in the ancient Near East. For St Paul it was natural that women should be subordinate to men in church as elsewhere.

Equally serious is the objection that according to the testimony of scripture God chose Jesus, a male, as the means of human salvation and was incarnate in a man. Jesus then chose only men as his disciples. All apostolic ministry in Bible and tradition comes through men. This is not a sociological observation, but is part of the scandal of particularity in revelation. This argument has been put particularly strongly by Dr. Graham Leonard, Bishop of London: 'I believe that the Scriptures speak of God as Father, that Christ was incarnate as a male. That he chose men to be his disciples in spite of breaking with tradition in his dealings with women, not because of social conditioning but because in the order of creation headship and authority is symbolically and fundamentally associated with maleness.'[11]

Though biblical precedents have always been taken seriously by Christians, they believe that they have been led by the Holy Spirit to interpret the whole biblical witness in the light of a deepening understanding of the gospel of love. The fundamental freedom and equality of the gospel, the realisation that in Christ there is neither Jew nor Greek, led early congregations to welcome gentiles and to abandon the traditional requirement that all priests should be of Jewish stock. With regard to the example of Jesus, since we are concerned with the service not of the dead Jesus but of the risen Christ, we cannot imitate the activities of Jesus in any sort of mechanical correspondence. Jesus today need not be inviting us to copy his actions in a past situation, but may be calling us to respond to the reality of new creation now.

Discussion of scripture has now inevitably taken us into further areas. There is the authority of tradition. We have already seen that assumptions of unbroken historical tradition in a literal sense are vulnerable to historical criticism at every stage. Tradition in the best sense is true to itself in its ability to be flexible and creative, rather than defensive and repetitive. We are not guarding a dead deposit, but hoping to serve the living God in his Church.

I turn now to the so-called theology of sexuality. Much opposition to women priests is based on arguments from Genesis, in which women are thought to be both secondary and the original source of sin, evil and temptation. But we may read Genesis as a meditation on the equality of men and women in creation. Life today in factories, schools, clubs, politics, is richer when lived together. This does not mean of course that the unmarried lives are less fully human and fulfilled than the married, or anything of that sort.

Coupled with the argument from orders of creation – always a highly dubious theological basis – is the theology of images. Christ the male image reflects the image of God the Father. But the Jesus Christ whom the church serves is not a kind of divinised male – this would indeed be idolatry.

It may be right that the symbolism of priesthood, as of the Church in general as God's servant for all mankind, should be as rich and comprehensive as possible, in representing not itself but Christ.

We come now to representation. Christ as man, it is often said, can alone represent man to God and God to man. Yet it is indeed a curious thought that a man can represent both men and women but a woman can only represent women.

Considering further the problem of representation brings me to the last of my areas of concern, that of ecumenical progress. It is always important to bear in mind the consequences of developments in churches for the oneness of the Church. Many churches, Lutheran, Reformed, Methodist, Disciples of Christ, have had ordained women in parish work for many years. In America the great majority of Christians have had women ministers in their denominations for years. In England and Spain this has not been the case. Different circumstances encouraged different natural reactions.

The Roman Catholic church is perhaps the most critical case in this area. Pope John Paul II has made his conservative position clear. Yet many Catholics would welcome the admission of women to priesthood on the same terms as men. On the question of representation, the best succinct argument I have found is from an editorial in the Jesuit periodical *The Month*:

> The point is often made that a priest needs to be a man because he represents Christ. But the real point is that in such a view of representation he represents Christ the redeemer; he does not impersonate Jesus of Nazareth. What is important is the sacrament in humanity, which men and women share.[12]

More difficult in the long term is the issue of the ordination of women in the orthodox churches, bound by the seven ecumenical councils. We need not say anything here to compound the severe difficulties faced by modern orthodox theologians. But it may be that in time employment of the traditional distinction between apostolic and ecclesiastical tradition will lead to movement on this issue as on others.

It can always be argued on this as on other issues that though agreement is possible in principle the time is not yet ripe for change. Precipitate action is always undesirable. But equally, it must be remembered that if the Church had waited always for the agreement of all its members, we should still be supporting slavery as well as its abolition.

Sometimes it is thought that the Church might graciously relax its rules against ordination as an act of forgiveness. On this at least we may all be agreed, that to be a woman is not to be *ipso facto* any more in need of forgiveness than to be a man.

10 Structuring elements of doctrine: the sacraments

SACRAMENTS

'Sacraments ordained by Christ be not only badges or tokens of Christian men's profession, but rather they be certain sure witnesses, and effectual signs of grace, and God's good will towards us, by the which he doth work invisibly in us, and doth not only quicken, but also strengthen and confirm our Faith in him.' So Article 25 of the Thirty Nine Articles.

In Chapter 7 we saw that most of the arguments in the Reformation discussion had been used before, but the alternatives were now shown up with a new sharpness. What was the relation, in the Lord's Supper, between the bread and wine and the body and blood of Christ? What did it mean to say 'This is my body', *hoc est corpus meum* (the Greek of course has no 'is', which is understood) which Luther scrawled in chalk on the table at Marburg? Was it just a sign (*hoc significat*), the position he attributed to Zwingli? Calvin produced the classic threefold structure of the signification, that is, the word of God's promise in the institution, the matter or substance, that is, the Christ with his death and resurrection, and the effect, that is, the benefits of Christ, the life in Christ (*Institutes* 4.17.1). Calvin's simple definition of a sacrament, borrowed from Augustine, that 'one may call it a testimony of divine grace towards us, confirmed by an outward sign, with mutual attestation of our piety towards him (*Inst.* 4.14.1) is continued, with an increasing stress on the symbolic nature of the testimony, in the history of the understanding of the sacraments thereafter.

SACRAMENTAL DOCTRINE

What then is the basis of a doctrine of the sacraments? In his short pamphlet on 'the Babylonian captivity of the Church' (Clemens

1.431.34f.), Luther says, 'If I were to follow the usage of scripture, I should say that there is only one sacrament, and three sacramental signs' (baptism, penance and the Lord's Supper) and in a later writing he could suggest that 'the sacred scriptures have only one sacrament, which is Christ the Lord himself (*Unum solum habent sacrae litterae sacramentum, quod est ipse Christus Dominus* (Disputatio de fide infusa et acquisita: *WA* 6.86.5f.).

In more recent times Edward Schillebeeckx writes of Christ as the primordial sacrament,[1] and Karl Barth has spoken of the birth of Christ as the one sacrament and of the human nature of Christ as the first sacrament.[2] This does not mean that baptism and communion then cease to be sacraments, but rather that they gain their meaning from their relation to Christ, who is the primary *sacramentum* or mystery of God. Similar views can be found in the work of Eberhard Jüngel.

Such an approach to the general term *sacramentum* appears to me to have much to commend it. It does not of course involve us in accepting what Barth or Luther then go on to say about baptism or eucharist in detail.

Jesus Christ, I would want to say, is the one sacrament of the Church in the primary sense. In his life the secret of God's will for men is made known in history and is effective in history. His being, which is the source of men's salvation, is the one *sacramentum fidei*. The communication of the nature of this salvation to men is the ministry of the word. Jesus comes into this world and calls for faith: to this corresponds the act of God and the response of men in the celebration of the sacrament of baptism. He already operates in the world as a living presence in the hearts of men. In the sacrament of communion a new awareness of this living presence becomes possible, and men and women respond in thanksgiving for the continuation of his presence in the world.

BAPTISM

Baptism and eucharist may now be understood in the light of the primary sacrament of Jesus Christ. Baptism comes into the New Testament with the baptism of John, which was probably founded on the rites of Jewish proselyte baptism. John prepares the people of God for God's coming. People repent, and receive forgiveness through a baptism by water. Jesus was baptised according to Matthew's theology to fulfil all righteousness, to assume the ministry of the servant of God. After Pentecost all who join the churches are baptised. This is the baptism of the spirit, as well as a water baptism. It marks repentance, but also the placing of the baptised in the household of God, the Christian community. Such baptism is a work of God which underlines the consequences for the world of the coming of Christ. It says, as it were, 'God has turned to men: come and turn to him.' The awareness of God is itself a product of what Jesus has achieved. The natural response of those who come is a renewal of repentance, as a reaction to the presence of God. God has come, therefore repent and join in his work.

Since baptism involves a coming to something that is already there, and not a creation of something through baptism, it need not be unreasonable to include in the household of faith the children of those who believe. In this way they may have the benefit of the influence of the Christian community in the years before they can make their own mature decisions. In fact, it seems unlikely that children were baptised in New Testament times – it is certainly unproven. Circumstances then were different. On the other hand, if people never think out the implications of their baptism or simply take this for granted, then they fail to take advantage of what has been done for them. The fact that some children may turn their backs on the values of an enlightened, affectionate and liberal upbringing is no good reason to abandon such values in the future. The disadvantages of infant baptism may be avoided by believers' baptism. Here the opposite danger may arise, of making the awareness of the presence of God apparently dependent on our moral effort and achievement. This need not of course always be the interpretation. It ought to be possible in particular circumstances to have the possibility of baptism at any age. What the Church has always found unacceptable is second baptism, doing it all over again. This is a sound policy. It may, however, be noted that various other practices, such as the proliferation in numerous denominations of various practically identical rites of ordination, come close to the same objection but have not met with similar condemnation.

EUCHARIST

There were of course in the Bible a number of precedents for the Lord's Supper. In Israel the significance of the Exodus from Egypt was celebrated by a solemn Paschal meal (Exod. 12) which was a pledge of the covenant to the chosen community of the people of God. In apocalyptic expectation too there was the hope of a messianic meal, reflected in the Lukan narrative in the promise of eating and drinking at Christ's table in heaven (22:28f.). The Lord's Supper contained in the communities of the early Church the elements of past and future, of memorial and anticipation. In the life and fate of Jesus the Passover found its fulfilment and end. Freedom from slavery is given not by the paschal lamb but by the lamb of God, who takes away the sins of the world. Christ our passover is sacrificed (1 Cor. 2:7) and his coming points to hope for the future. As often as you eat this bread and drink this cup you proclaim the Lord's death till he comes. (1 Cor. 11:26).

It is particularly in St John's gospel of course that the sacramental significance of the so-called real presence is most strikingly worked out. 'I am the bread of life.' 'I am the living bread from heaven.' 'Unless you eat the flesh of the son of man and drink his blood you have no life in you.' (John 6:52f.). Yet the same writer can use phrases like 'I am the door', 'I am the vine.' 'It is the spirit that gives life, the flesh is of no avail.' Realism is evidently not intended to be literal description. St Paul too can ask, 'The cup of blessing which we bless, is it not a means of sharing in the blood of Christ? The bread which we break, is it not a participation in the body of Christ?' The breaking of bread is integrally related to sharing in the body of Christ. 'Because there is one loaf we, many as we are, are one body.' (1 Cor. 10.16f.).

What precisely happened at the Last Supper, or when it happened, appears not to be clear from the evidence available. There is an important school of exegetical thought which concludes that the meal in fact never took place. This is however usually combined with a theology for which the sacraments are in any case superfluous. That a meal of some kind took place seems likely from the fact that the early communities had a meal and related it to Jesus' meal. In their meals and in their liturgies they had the experience of a deepening of faith, of a new awareness of the presence of Christ which helped them in living as Christians. This has continued to happen where men and women have celebrated the Lord's Supper. The basis of the celebration remains however not the Last Supper as such, but Jesus' whole act of communion with men in incarnation and atonement.

The eucharist was understood, as we have seen, in different ways in different early communities. For the West, Augustine summed it up in the famous phrase '*verbum visibile*', the visible word, which complements the *verbum audibile*, or the word which is heard.[3] Perhaps we could sum up the meaning of the eucharist in the following way.

In the first instance the eucharist is a memorial, a recalling in the most deliberate manner of the life and passion of Christ. Secondly, it is an expression and anticipation of the hope that some day we shall all reach the fulfilment of God's purpose for us in Christ, when like him we shall be with God in the fullest sense. Thirdly it is the means by which we may receive through faith a heightened awareness of the presence of Christ in the world and in our own lives as Christians. Christ is always present with us. Here we may receive a new and fresh vision of the ultimate reality of his presence. There is nothing magic or material in this awareness. But particularly in the absence of an object of empirical perception we may come to understand again, perhaps as nowhere else, the meaning of the love of God in Christ. Fourthly, we know this love particularly in the sharing of the bread and wine in community. The eucharist is a focal point of the Christian life for others. Here we may recall Luther's comment. A Christian lives in Christ through faith, and in his neighbour through love. Last and not least important, eucharist, thanksgiving, is an occasion for giving thanks to God in prayer for the presence of the risen Christ within this world, for the first fruits of that which is to come.

Understood in this way, eucharist and baptism, as expressions of Christ the sacrament, are particular and concrete manifestations of the proclamation of the word, which is word of Christ. Word and sacrament are not rival means of grace but reflect different aspects of the engagement of God in his own nature with history through Jesus Christ, and the development of that relationship through the Holy Spirit.

11 The Church in Christian community

THEORY AND PRACTICE

From the structuring elements of doctrine we must turn to the further description of the nature of the Church as the Church of the love of God in practice. Theory and practice are interrelated and equally important. The theory may be impeccable, but if it is divorced from considerations of practice it may be of no avail. Many a Christian community has had theoretically impeccable theological credentials, and yet has failed lamentably by any standards in practice. Sometimes it is the other way round, and this is a much healthier state of affairs. But in the long term, clear thinking has never done anyone any great harm. It is vital to work out a theoretical basis for understanding the structuring elements of the Church, as different situations throw up theoretical problems in different ways.

In looking at the wider implications of understanding the Church as the Church of the love of God, we may concentrate on four main issues. I shall summarise them for convenience under the four headings of attention, thanksgiving, forgiveness and reconciliation. All are of course related. Let me spell out briefly what I have in mind.

The basic characteristic of a Church which is grounded in God's love must be attention to the source of its life in God. This means openness, listening, hearing, looking, being responsible to and waiting for the message of the gospel. If the gospel is invitation it is an invitation which must be awaited and taken up. Listening to the word, being open to divine being, awaiting the vision of the presence – there are many ways of imagining this dimension. A Church may be ever so forgiving, reconciling, caring, but unless it constantly attends to the love of God, allows its love to be rekindled and its faith to be inspired by the source of God's love in Christ, then it rapidly becomes yet another minor voluntary social organisation. I have the greatest possible respect for voluntary social organisations. But a Church which provides only this role for its members speedily kills faith and dies from the sheer unremitting boredom of its worship. Attention, then, is crucial.

Thanksgiving is related to attention. The Church of the love of God is so only through being related to its source, and will want to recall itself to its basis in constant thanksgiving. Here we come again to prayer and worship as part of the attention of the Church. A Church which has no sense of thanksgiving is likely to find itself speedily in despair before the mundane problems of life in community, and so to become incapable of thought and action. This leads again to boredom, and a boring Church is of no use, either to itself or to its neighbours.

Forgiveness is related to attention and to thanksgiving. The Church is the community of salvation, of those saved, being saved and to be saved through God's grace, for which the Church waits, gives thanks and exists. In human life we are constantly exercising pressures on one another, as individuals and as community, sometimes for better and sometimes for worse. Injustices are done between individuals and between communities. As individuals and as communities we have much for which to repent, much for which to forgive one another and to seek forgiveness. Repentance and forgiveness are not exactly the most obvious factors at work in the political, economic and social life of the twentieth century. Here is an area where the Church, based on God's forgiving love, may do something for its own life and for the life of our common humanity.

Fourth and last is the dimension of reconciliation. The basis of the Church is the gospel of reconciliation between God and man, between men and men, through Jesus Christ. Reconciliation between individuals, between Christian communities, between peoples of the world, is of the essence of the promise of God's kingdom. Christians in community have often been notoriously divisive, whether in social, political, theological or other areas. The response to divisiveness is not dull uniformity, but reconciliation in which diverse perspectives and life-styles are reconciled on the basis of the character of God's love as revealed in Jesus Christ. Here, if anywhere, theoretical structures of the Church must be constantly related to social and political realities.

COMMITMENT IN COMMUNITY

We may deal now with each of these features, in regard first to Christians in community, then to Christians as individuals, and then to the wider context of the Church in society. We come first to the Church in Christian community.

The Church, we agreed with the tradition, is one, holy, catholic and apostolic, at least in eschatological perspective. These marks of the Church are based in its source in the love of God. Perhaps we can look again at this oneness, this unity. We may also look at oneness in terms of attention, thanksgiving, forgiveness and reconciliation. The oneness of the Church is based not on any organisational monolithicity but on attention to the gospel which is its source. This does not mean that one can for example use christological models from the New Testament in any kind of one-to-one correspondence with Church structure. I have written elsewhere on the uses of the category of parable in the doctrine of scripture, and this applies also to the Church.[1] Though parable is always relevant, not everything is parabolic, or in the same way parabolic. But, as in the central parable of the vine, the branches are always dependent on the main plant. It is in the life, death and resurrection of Jesus, new creation fulfilling creation, that the oneness of the Church is based.

Commitment to the oneness of the Church means commitment to the ecumenical movement. This is not of course self-evident, for it could be and often is argued that oneness might include a purely invisible and spiritual unity, in which other denominations are excluded from the Church, and a few individuals outside the chosen flock are included only in virtue of God's hidden grace. In my own view, the practical realisation of oneness must imply concrete co-operation and the quest for organisational unity. Such unity need not limit the basic freedom of Christians to respond to God in a great variety of different ways.

There are further serious arguments against ecumenical movements. Some of these, as we have seen, have proved amply justified. Sometimes ecumenism is simply a disguised form of ecclesiastical imperialism, in which large or socially privileged Christian groups seek to take over weaker organisations, with scant regard for their distinctive traditions. Perhaps more serious than interdenominational sabre-rattling is the distraction from the pastoral work of the Church in the modern world which arises from internal preoccupation with ecumenical issues. It is easier, and much more congenial, to join a round of ecumenical conferences from Hungary to Honolulu than to get involved in the grinding routine of inner city mission or intellectual engagement with contemporary thought. *Oekumene* forms its own family gatherings and clusters of patronage, even unto children's children.

It is clear that, like all human activity, ecumenical work has its shortcomings, and these have to be consciously avoided. But still the scandal of disunity is a serious weakness of Christianity, and it is theologically indefensible. Concern for unity may lead to papering over differences in undue haste. Concern for truth is always prior, and unity is not to be sought at any price. But all truth is one in Christ, and the ecumenical question is always before us.

How far is our own conception of truth based simply on custom, however venerable, and on prejudice, however sophisticated? In such matters the Churches of traditional Christianity in Europe are especially lumbered with tradition, and may need to learn from the younger Churches of Africa and Asia. But tradition may also be a source of flexibility and imaginative growth, while the enthusiasms of the younger Churches sometimes turn out to be simply a reflection of the concerns of the older Churches, echoes rather than new developments.

In ecumenical theology it often turns out that differences in opinion cut across denominations. In practice it may be necessary to engage in symbolic acts of common commitment, its intercommunion, before formal union of organisational structure and theological confession takes place. In any case, there are churches in which there has never been formal allegiance to a single statement or confession, and the question of confessional authority is likely to reflect changing understandings of authority in general at different periods in history. Co-operation in social, pastoral and educational work is one well-proven way of learning to share with other sorts of Christians and making a common witness in a given community.

We said that ecumenism could not be pursued at the expense of truth, but only for the sake of truth. Time must be allowed for any radical social adjustment, and haste may provoke disappointment and cynicism. But deliberation is one thing and procrastination is another. As Avery Dulles put it recently, the churches are still dragging their feet when it comes to ecumenism.

Oneness means then attention to the gospel, and thanksgiving for the opportunity of making a Christian contribution to the unity of mankind through the unity of different confessions and indeed of different races in the Church. It means forgiveness, as unity overcomes the bitterness caused by a multitude of wrongs done between Christians in the name of God. It means reconciliation, as people of different persuasions accept each other's integrity and seek to understand each other in freedom and love. In the face of the history of religious persecution we may despair of such words as freedom and love. But such despair would be a last tribute to the persecutors of history.

An ecumenical Church ought to be free from the crippling influence of nationalist prejudice. Though not necessarily a 'free church', it ought to be free from state control. But it would be strange if churches in different countries did not continue to reflect, within their overall Christian unity, distinctive features of worship and policy deriving from their old traditions. I see no reason why there should not be episcopal churches in some areas and non-episcopal in others, with different understandings of ministry reflected in different areas, just as in other areas of life in community there is a variety of practice. There might quite properly be different understandings of the ministerial function of the Bishop of Rome in different parts of the Church, within the fabric of a greater Christian union. Such a vision will doubtless bring shudders to the minds of traditional Roman Catholics and traditional Protestants alike. But our seventeenth-century ancestors would have been astonished at the thought of breakfast in New York followed by lunch in Frankfurt, instant television coverage around the world, and many other things we take as a matter of course.

MARKS OF COMMUNITY

I come now to holiness as a characteristic of Christian community. It is notoriously difficult to write a novel about a perfectly good man, and it is perhaps equally difficult to describe a perfectly holy man. Such a person must not only be perfectly good but must also be perfectly devoted to God. But since for New Testament Christianity our righteousness is hidden with God in Christ, the perfectly holy man, like Plato's perfectly good man, may be hidden from public recognition, and the perfectly unholy man may appear to be the paragon of righteousness. At the same time, this paradoxical attitude to virtues can clearly be taken too far. Presumably it is not open to us to pursue true holiness by taking an attitude to life which is as outwardly selfish, brutal towards others and dissolute as possible.

How then may we conceive of the holiness of the Church in Christian community? To be holy is to be a faithful disciple of Jesus Christ. Discipleship is focussed for many people by the notion of the imitation of Christ, *imitatio Christi*. Since we worship the living Christ rather than the dead Jesus, *imitatio* need not be conceived of in the narrow sense of reflecting the actions of Jesus, even assuming that we had a photographic guide to these.

Yet certain structuring elements in the gospel of the life of Jesus remain focal for us. Where we abandon these, history appears to show that Christianity goes wrong. Through the New Testament narratives there comes a picture of a man of absolute integrity, completely devoted to God and completely and selflessly devoted to his fellow men, a man with a mission, in teaching and action, in the service of the coming Kingdom of God. If he had been less than this we might think it unlikely that he would have been worshipped as divine and human. If he were shown by research to have been beyond all reasonable doubt a man who corrupted his fellows, exploiting them in ways great and small, mean and small-minded, then we should certainly not be justified in continuing to put him at the centre of our faith. It is this integrity, this faithfulness unto death, which has inspired holiness in the Christian community through the ages. Other men have of course been holy. But in the case of Jesus, Christians have been enabled by the power of the Holy Spirit to show holiness and faithfulness in ways which have surprised none more than themselves.

Holiness, in this apostolic sense, is produced not through deliberate spiritual engineering but through attention, thanksgiving, forgiveness and reconciliation. It just continues to happen, and so to encourage the rest of us to be a little more attentive.

One, holy – what are we to say of the catholicity of the Church in community? Blessed are the narrow-minded, for theirs is the kingdom of heaven. Blessed are the empty-minded, for theirs is the kingdom of heaven. It seems sometimes that Christians are either narrow-minded, and so the most prejudiced and limited of creatures, or else they are empty-minded, endlessly open to all possibilities, so afraid of being thought judgemental that they have no means of assessing what is preferable and what is to be avoided in the Church. Catholicity means that the Church must be able to embrace all sorts and conditions of men and women. It is truly concerned for fellowship with all men on an equal basis, regardless of colour, race or creed, regardless of social class or other distinction. In Christ there is neither Jew nor Greek, black nor white. This does not mean that there are not human activities and opinions of which the Church will disapprove. Love means intolerance of hatred and evil, opposition to any sort of exploitation by one group or individual of other groups or individuals.

But the challenge of catholicity remains a standing challenge to parochialism, elitism, inverted snobbery and the like. This has implications for the Church within society as a whole. But if charity begins at home, it has devastating implications for relations within Christian congregations and denominations and for ecumenical dialogue. If we are prepared to love only those who share our own particular theology, churchmanship and social manners then we are reflecting no more than the sense of self-preservation within their own kind shown by most living species. What do ye more than others? As elsewhere, catholicity means constant attention to the centre of God's love. It means thanksgiving, forgiveness and reconciliation.

The last of the four great attributes of the Church is apostolicity. The Church is called to proclaim the gospel in its life and work, to carry on the tradition of communicating the faith in word and action. It is easy to despair of the Church. And yet despair, we said, is a kind of tribute to the victory of evil in the world. Apostolicity, apparently such an old-fashioned sounding virtue, is nowhere more necessary than in the modern secular world. Here too attention to the source of grace in God's love, thanksgiving for grace often despite the appearance of things, forgiveness and especially consciousness of things for which we ourselves are in need of forgiveness, reconciliation on the basis of the love of God through Jesus Christ – these are the requirements. If we fail here then we are like those who hide their lights under bushels and are unprofitable servants. Of course we all fail, again and again, but we may still be used as the instruments of God's apostolic love.

Such a brief survey of course comes nowhere near a comprehensive account of the roles of Christians in community. But it perhaps offers a few signals of direction, to be filled out in different ways in different local situations. It will have been noticed that the description of what may be possible varies between the confident and the less optimistic. The Church participates in the eternal communion of saints, but is not herself the realisation of that communion. *Communio sanctorum* is a powerful and helpful symbol of Christian self-understanding. But it may easily be romanticised so as to focus on a spiritual elite and lead us to despair of the ordinary Christian community in its daily existence. The Church is also the pilgrim people of God, triumphing often precisely where it seems to fail.

LOVE AND FREEDOM

In thinking of the Church in community I have tried throughout this chapter to indicate unqualified support for ecumenical theology, and I would in no way wish to retreat from that position. However, I think it appropriate to end this section on a note of caution.

We have been thinking of the danger of romanticism in speaking of the *communio sanctorum*. Nowhere is this a greater danger than in ecumenical theology. The quest for unity, wholeness, continuity with the whole past tradition, can never be achieved at the cost of truth. This is particularly the case where the standard of truth is the self-giving love of God in Jesus Christ, with all that this implies in concern for individual persons, and for small communities within larger communities. Karl Barth characterised God as the God of Jesus Christ who loves in freedom.[2] Love and freedom, freedom for others, freedom intellectual, social and political, not for itself but for the service of God and man, go together.

A proper understanding of the dialectical relationship between love and freedom is not the prerogative of any one denomination. Bigotry has been and is pretty evenly spread among Catholics, Protestants and others. It seems to me however to be important to remember, precisely in ecumenical theology, that Protestants have every reason to rejoice still in the Reformation, because it represents a basic return to Christian freedom in love in numerous directions. Without the Reformation our understanding of the gospel would be impoverished, and life in society today would doubtless be much less free. For all its faults, too, the liberal Protestant tradition which arose from the Reformation is quite as much part of the precious heritage of the gospel as the work of the early fathers. The same must apply, for different reasons and with similar reservations, to the evangelical tradition in the Protestant churches.

On the other hand, Catholics may rejoice in the Reformation because it paved the way for and strengthened those parts of the tradition which were to lead to the fresh perspectives of Vatican II, in many ways the most daring of Christian self-examinations of our time, and the changes which have arisen from this – an event from which Protestants might learn.

But there are signs in these days, in both Catholicism and Protestantism, of a return to the fortress mentality of the middle ages or the post-Reformation period. In my view there is no point whatever in returning to an apostolic consensus where this may involve decisions affecting the freedom and welfare, physical and mental, of individual societies, which are contrary to the appropriate Christian response to the God of love. It is important here to be entirely frank. Much as one may be grateful for his stand on such issues as peace and reconciliation, it appears to me that there is in much of the moral and social teaching of Pope John Paul II a serious barrier to ecumenical progress. The same applies to much of the moral and social teaching of the Orthodox churches. There are of course similar viewpoints in Protestant denominations, for example over-zealous commitment to an infallible and inerrant Bible. But the consequences in Roman Catholicism are particularly serious, because of the direct exercise of papal power, clearly seen in such comparatively minor matters as the immediate cessation of the laicisation of priests, and related issues.

Such policies affect seriously the life of Christians in community, in such matters as clerical celibacy, and the role of women in the Church. Though changes can only arise from within, it can be no help to minorities, Catholic, Orthodox, or Protestants, if their fellows in other denominations appear to embrace these developments with ecumenical fervour. But these decisions also have, in the case of issues like birth control, devastating effects on family life throughout society. In my own view it goes without saying that it will always be impossible to purchase the luxury of apostolic fellowship in the eucharist at the expense of misery for hundreds of millions, yet unborn throughout the world. Such thoughts are unpalatable. But they are also inevitable, if the Church exists in God's providence for the service of all mankind, and not mankind for the convenience of the Church.

12 The life of the individual and the Church

INDIVIDUALS

We shall look now at the role of the Church in relation to the life of the individual Christian. One cannot be a Christian in complete isolation from the life of the Christian community without serious loss. There is the constant danger of distortion, preciosity, and introversion. But equally, no man can believe for another. The existential dimension, the dimension of personal responsibility for what we believe and personal faith, is vital. Unless we may be able to understand our own lives as sustained, at least at some crucial times, by the gift of personal faith, then there is indeed something very odd about the relation between the promise and the fulfilment of the gospel. This fulfilment is eschatological, and may be preceded by the dark night of the soul. But we should not despair too readily, perhaps, of the centrality and the infinite wonder of personal faith, and its implications in Christian life and work.

The Apostles' Creed speaks of the community of the Church and then of the forgiveness of sins. It is often said that the Christian life begins with repentance, the conviction of sin, and the awareness of the forgiveness of sins, and there is something to be said for this. The message of John the Baptist was a call to repentance. Jesus, too, according to the first evangelist, began after his temptation in the wilderness to proclaim the message, 'Repent, for the kingdom of heaven is at hand.' Much preaching has followed this pattern. First comes analysis of the condition of man, his alienation from his neighbours and himself, his feelings of anxiety and insecurity, and then the answer is sought in the gospel. This approach has the advantage of beginning where man is, and then speaking of God. It was used to brilliant effect in Paul Tillich's answering theology. But it also poses problems. Bonhoeffer spoke of the unsatisfactory nature of a 'sniffing out of men's sins' in order then to bring the gospel to bear on them. The Christian faith is from the beginning good news, and invitation to a fuller life, to new humanity as co-humanity in the love of God through Jesus Christ. For many people attention to the gospel will be something which they grew up to consider more deeply, but into which they were baptised, within the family and community of faith. For others it will be a more or less sudden breakthrough, but again it will be in contact with the message through men and women who live as those who have faith.

To this extent however, the stress on repentance is entirely right, namely that reflection on the bearer of the message and the means of salvation, the life and fate of Jesus, must bring with it aversion to all that is in contrast to the life of Jesus in our own lives. It was because men were more like us than like him, that he had to suffer. It is only and precisely when we see the reality of the love of God in Christ that we see how, for all our correctness and morality, we are much in need of forgiveness.

Here too, and this is one of the continuing factors in the dynamic of the Christian life, this is an experience which needs constantly to be renewed. As men and women realise the need for forgiveness they know that in Christ their sins have been forgiven. This is the strangeness of the love of Christ, that his love is utterly without limits, without reservations, reaching and enveloping all.

The Christian life then begins and continues in recognition and gratitude, in attention and thanksgiving, which involves at the same time repentance. Forgiveness is related to reconciliation as the gratitude of the individual is related to the sacrifice of the atonement.

Here we come to the doctrine which, for the Lutheran branch of the Church at least, is and always has been the centre of the gospel, the doctrine of justification by faith. The terminology is of course borrowed from St Paul. As men and women before God we know that we are far from righteous, just, holy, loving, as God is righteous, just, holy, loving. We realise that between the holiness and love of God and our estrangement there is a great gulf, a real distance. Yet we know that God has accepted us, the acceptance of the unacceptable. He has come to us with his grace, through the reconciliation made between love and justice in the life and fate of Jesus Christ. This is the awareness of justification. Much ink, even blood, has been spilled over the question of whether this is simply a declaring just, despite our actual unworthiness, or a real making just. The answer would seem to be that it involves both. It is a real and not a fictional acceptance, a real making just. But though it is a permanent character, its continuing significance depends on whether it is constantly renewed in trust in and commitment to God, and in the kind of life that this implies.

But that justification is in the first or later instances dependent on our good works. We have none, at least none comparable to what we lack. To that extent it is obviously justification by faith alone, by grace alone, solely on the basis of what Christ has done for us. Again, central as the principle of *sola fide* is, it cannot be applied by analogy in every detail of Christian theology. It is not necessarily always the centre of the gospel. On the basis of the principle of faith alone it is sometimes said that it is improper to seek reasonable grounds for faith. We believe because it is impossible. Yet however we may stress the doctrine of justification, it is certainly not an invitation, much less a command, to believe a dozen impossible things every morning before breakfast.

FAITH, HOPE AND LOVE

Justification, then, is not the result but the presupposition of the Christian life, though it is an awareness that needs constant reminder and renewal. With this renewal goes hand in hand another aspect of the life of faith, that traditionally called sanctification, growth and progress in the Christian life.

Sanctification we can look at primarily in terms of two features. These are summed up in Martin Luther's brilliant epigram: 'A Christian lives in Christ through faith, and in his neighbour through love.' (This is taken from his short essay 'On Christian Freedom', which should perhaps be required reading for every Christian). Progress in the Christian life should involve a constant deepening of faith. Faith may be deepened through meditation, through reasoning, through thinking, through doubts and struggle with doubts, through life in society among Christians and non-Christians alike. To quote Luther again, he said that a theologian is made not through listening to lectures and reading books, but by living and dying and being damned. This applies clearly to every Christian life. It is always part of faith's commitment to seek to gain a deeper understanding of itself and of its grounds, and to seek a deeper level of discipleship. Devotion to God is not, perhaps, one of the most fashionable of modern theological topics. But if it is not central, nothing else can be of value. Life in Christ through faith, and in one's neighbour through love – John McLeod Campbell said that no one can understand the Fatherhood of God who does not understand the brotherhood of man.[1] If I have faith to move mountains, and have not love, then, as St Paul put it, that's not really much good. I shall not attempt here to go into the nature of Christian love except to recall that it is in all cases the exact opposite of sentimentality. It means concrete identification with all the concerns and needs of men. Otherwise, as the New Testament reminds us, 'I was in prison and you did not visit me'. Such a concern is clearly not limited to the members of the Christian community.

The Christian faith also includes love of God. This may seem obvious, and yet it is strange how little many Protestant theologians have had to say about love for God. Love for God is not of course any sort of danger to the principle of justification by faith. It is not that we can level by any purely natural capacity. But love as response, response to him who first loved us, ought to be a natural and deepening expression of Christian faith. So much in Protestantism has been purely intellectual. We are prepared to have a grim faith in God, to reason, to believe. But any talk of love for God, of a warm affection for God, seems to smack of pietism. If affection is stifled long enough it will grow cold. I don't myself think it a precondition of being a modern man that the love of God should be discouraged.

A third main category of the Christian life along with faith and love is traditionally that of hope. Hope is orientated towards the future. It relates to things which are thought desirable, which there are grounds to expect but which are not yet realised, the details of which remain to some extent uncertain. Christian hope extends beyond the life of faith in the present. It looks forward to the completion of the work of creation and reconciliation when Christ shall be all in all. Because it goes beyond this world, it does not regard the way things are here, all the imperfection and suffering as well as the good, as God's final consummation of things. Because it hopes and believes that even now God's spirit is working in the world, it does not rest content with the way things are, but seeks to transform society in obedience to Christ, neither confusing its faith with knowledge of God's will, nor abandoning the world here and now to its fate. What hope, which is rooted in faith and acted on in love, means for the relationship between the Christian and society, we shall want to consider in the next chapter.

DEATH AND LIFE

To return to the creed, we may notice that it speaks in one breath, as it were, of the forgiveness of sins, the resurrection of the body, and the life everlasting. Here we come again to the eschatological dimension of the Church: the Church of the love of God is concerned for the welfare of individuals and of communities in this life and beyond. When the bridge of physical continuity is gone, the love of God upholds us before, through and after death. The Christian life begins with the gospel of salvation and goes on for ever.

Death is for us the most final of all measurements, and in the modern world it is increasingly hard for us to think of any meaningful sort of future for men after death. In the ancient world, particularly in the context of Hellenistic-Jewish apocalyptic expectation, such a notion was not hard to envisage. Jesus himself, New Testament scholarship has shown, most probably expected the imminent end of the world, when God's kingdom would break in suddenly by divine intervention. What are we to expect to happen to us after death? What are we to say, too, of the future of the whole universe, which Christian faith affirms to have been created by God? It is of course possible to take a short course with regard to the individual, as in some variations of the 'realised eschatology theme'. As the individual comes to terms with the fact that some day he must die, and lives in affirmation of the value of his own life at every present moment, lives that is to say existentially, then he is laying hold now of eternal life. But this does not solve the cosmic problem of the destiny of the universe. It could be, too, that there might be a fulfilment of the destiny of man which would not necessarily involve the end of the world in time. The world could go on, while the future of man was being completed. However that may be, we in this life are unable by definition and constitution to understand or imagine what life in a non-temporal dimension, after death, would be like. The idea of a non-temporal continuation of temporal states might not add up to eternity, freedom from all the conditions of the temporal.

We shall say little more here of the Christian hope.[2] But it is important to remember that the love of God in the individual Christian, in the community and in society has a future as well as a past and a present. The creed continues to speak of this future in terms of the resurrection of the body. Both the Hebrew notion of the resurrection of the flesh and the Greek notion of the immortality of the soul indicate that it is not just part of a man, but that which constitutes his essential humanity, which is to be restored. This would appear to involve the personality of the individual after the disintegration of the brain. How personal identity could be continued is hard to say. But certainly the idea of the absorption of all individuality into God's being would appear to suggest a future unlike that which Christian knowledge of God's concern with real relationships would suggest.

The New Testament speaks of the goal of the Christian life as adoption with Christ into sonship, into the life of God. This is everlasting life, and involves a new understanding of God's presence. For those who have faith, says St Paul, nothing can separate us from the love of Christ. This is heaven; it is eternal life. Since God's love in Christ, unlike ours, is boundless, it seems inconceivable that the door to eternal love will ever be closed. Notions of purgatory appear to be an unnecessary solution to some genuine but mistaken dilemmas of medieval theology.

The life of the Christian, as an individual and in community, runs on into the Kingdom of God, the last of these eschatological concepts which we shall notice. The Kingdom is God's consummation in Christ of all his work in creation. In Jesus it has already broken in, but is still not completed. It is built up by the Spirit, and will finally be completed by God in a new way. Meanwhile Christians, who hope for this completion, may work in ways that will assist rather than hinder the bringing in of the Kingdom. The Kingdom has a future in which the present realities of this world may be radically changed. But before this, and integral to this, it involves the transformation of this present world, even if the task is to be full of setbacks and disasters. The nature of this present eschatological task within the temporal dimension will concern us now in thinking of the Church in society. This area also involves the whole question of Christian ethics as individual and social ethics. But such a study needs to be treated by itself, if we are to begin to do justice to the issues, and cannot be entered upon here.

13 The Church in society

NEW CREATION AND NEW SOCIETY

We have been thinking of the life of the Christian as an individual and as a member of the Christian community. We turn now more explicitly to the role of the Church in society. We look first at the more institutional, and then at the more individual aspects of Christian faith in society.

New creation in Jesus Christ is at once the fulfilment and the transformation of the old creation. The Churches' role is to be an instrument of the love of God for all mankind. It becomes clear that the work of the Church in society is central to its existence. Its role of preaching and teaching, building up Christian community, we have already considered. But beyond this it has always worked in all kinds of directions. The way in which the institutional Church works in society will be determined partly by its particular structure in different areas, and by its understanding of itself as Christian community. Different understandings have different advantages and disadvantages.

We may think of Karl Barth's vision of the Church under the Word and often *contra mundum*, Schleiermacher's of the community of individuals aware of the consciousness of absolute dependence, Hegel's of the empirical Church as the spiritual community,[1] Bonhoeffer's of the communion of saints. If we think of what was perhaps *the* great crisis of relations between Christians and the state in this century, the Christian resistance to Hitler in Germany, we find a great variety of perspectives, in the kerygmatic tradition of Karl Barth's circle, the old liberal Protestant tradition in Von Soden and others, the Catholic resistance in the White Rose group in Munich, the Lutheran pietism of Von Möltke and many of the Kreisau circle, the Christian humanism of Bonhoeffer's last letters. Other people with similar backgrounds took the line of collaboration with Nazism. Such is the reality of human frailty.

It might be thought that the answer to the compromising of Christian standards is the separation, as far as possible, of Church and society. There is of course a long tradition of such separation, from the monastic movements to the Free Churches, a tradition which has often been a lonely witness to the gospel in times of compromise and double standards. Where the state has sought to control the internal affairs of the Church, thus threatening the autonomy of its preaching, teaching and pastoral care, the Church has always felt it necessary to resist. A classic case is the controversy leading up to the Scottish Disruption and the founding of the Free Church of Scotland in 1843.

In such conflicts, however, there is often a heavy price to be paid for freedom. Those in 1843 who remained within the Old Church felt that Christian community required intimate ties with the whole social and institutional structure of the society in which the gospel was to be preached and lived. Christians have always found it relatively easy, though humanly costly, to work out ways of resistance to the state and to society for the sake of the gospel. It is more difficult to work out appropriate ways of building bridges between Christian community and society, and of engaging in the right sort of construction between Christianity and culture.

How to live in the world without being worldly, to love one's fellow men and live completely in secular society without losing touch with the gospel, this is less than simple. In the Europe of the mid-twentieth century the Barthian theology which had provided such a vital and wonderful basis for resistance to Nazism proved peculiarly helpless before the need for construction and for Christian leadership in pointing to the structures of a new society after the second world war. Those who stayed with Barth often developed a fortress mentality and refused to move with the times, thereby losing great opportunities for the Church in a new age. Those who abandoned Barth lost much that could have provided substance for new reconstruction, and proved equally ineffectual. Other movements provided similar reactions, illustrating the reality of the problem of constructive thinking about Church and society.

Modern society is of course endlessly complex, and complicated in different ways in different continents. We are no longer concerned with blueprints for relations between Church and society in a village economy in a small area of Europe, as classical theology often was. In the face of such complexity it is coming to be recognised as impossible to produce a global theology which will deal with all aspects of the relations between Church and society. It should however be possible to produce a reasoned case for a programme of guiding principles, illustrated by appropriate selected examples. Such a programme can scarcely be of definitive status for the future. But it may be hoped, by reflecting the experience of the past and the present, to make a contribution towards the development and implementation of future programmes.

LOVE AGAINST EVIL

We have seen examples of the interference of the state in the affairs of the Church. But what of the interference of the Church in the affairs of the state? How far may the Church become involved, and how may this best be done? The Christian gospel is of God's love for all men. Where there is exploitation by men of their fellow men and women, the love of God implies intolerance of evil and exploitation. The obvious issue here is human rights. Where the state infringes or denies human rights, Christians are bound to respond. But may they do this only as individuals, perhaps in connection with the work of Amnesty International? Should not the Church keep out of politics?

Christian involvement in politics has often been disastrous, as the Church has lent its support and blessing to numerous dubious regimes in history. The New Testament communities, it may be said, were not involved in politics. But of course at that period Christianity was more like a private society than a thread interwoven in the fabric of a complex civilisation.

Where human rights are infringed the Church has a duty to speak out. If the shameful lessons of the world's attitudes to the Jews of Europe in the 1930s and '40s are not to be forgotten then it is imperative that infringement of human rights should be firmly opposed by the Churches. Such recent tragedies as the mass starvation in Cambodia only serve to underline the point. Of course influence brings responsibility. Those who start popular movements must be prepared to reflect on the consequences, sometimes not for themselves but for others, which impetuous action may bring. But the basic principle is clear.

It may be said that poor housing in one area is just as much an infringement of human rights as press censorship and imprisonment in another. All are compromised, and so none need be expressly condemned. But though *all* denials of human rights are clearly to be condemned, there are vast and crucial differences, as between murder and parking offences. If the case of individual human rights is reasonably clear, what of the individual rights of those killed in war? There is little hint in the war sermons cheerfully uttered on both sides in the first world war of the millions whose human rights ended abruptly in the trenches in a few months of 1916. Even if wars may be inevitable in some circumstances, always sinful but sometimes inevitable, does the Christian then have to acquiesce in all wars? We may think of the resistance of the Berrigan brothers to the Vietnam war in recent years.

CHURCH AND POLITICS

The primary task of the Church is to preach the gospel in word and action, and not to get involved directly in politics. Its political comments are often hopelessly naive and its actions ill-advised, because politics is not its professional competence. Politics ought to be left to the politicians, who, it may be hoped, will be open to Christian conviction. The theocratic pretensions of the Church in the past have led to much human suffering. This applies not only to Christianity but to Islam and the other major religions.

But what if the politicians are themselves corrupt? It will not do to exemplify Christian naivety by condemning political comments by churchmen and then producing a supposedly neutral but in fact highly politicised manifesto in reply.[2]

We spoke of the terrible record of the Churches and of European civilisation regarding the Jews. The Jewish people must be regarded as a privileged people of God, to whom mankind owes an unparalleled debt. This does not mean that all activities of Jewish organisations need always be approved of, but it does mean that reconstruction of relations ought to follow centuries of prejudice.

The need for reappraisal is also necessary in relation to other religions. As the example of the work of Canon Kenneth Cragg shows, appreciation of other religions need not detract in the least from deeply held Christian convictions.[3] Appreciation need not be uncritical. But particularly in the light of growing racism in the world, there is need as never before for mutual understanding and appreciation.

We would not wish simply to suggest that the Churches must join with the religious in society against the non-religious. Such a stance, far from promoting the unity of mankind, would be likely only to hinder it. The religious and the transcendent are ambivalent values, and whilst necessary to the understanding of God, are by no means sufficient. Our world is increasingly a world of humanists, agnostics and atheists. Modern culture is largely an agnostic culture. Many of the people who are most concerned for the welfare of mankind have no religious convictions. On an intellectual plane, questions of truth and meaning in existence and in the future of society may sometimes be shared more deeply between Christians and non-Christians than among the religious.

SCIENCE

The question of the nature of the best relationships between Church and society, or between Church and culture, is both fundamental and difficult. A further aspect of the issue may be seen in considering the churches' attitudes to modern science. Science has brought enormous benefits to man. Knowledge once achieved will not go away. Modern scientific culture raises sharp questions of intellectual justification for religions. Though there are in modern culture outbreaks of resistance to science and turning to transcendental meditation and the like, it seems clear that assimilation of questions about the nature of truth, meaning and reality of the sort familiar to the western world will eventually take place throughout the world, bringing critical and agnostic attitudes to God as they travel.

Of course nineteenth-century scientific positivism is philosophically untenable, and scientists recognise that their views are culturally relative as much as those of others. But the recognition of the complexity of cultural relativity, and the fundamental critical attitude produced by the European Enlightenment, are likely to stay as long as a totalitarian understanding of thought, of the sort envisaged by Orwell's *1984*, is avoided.

Some theologians have seen science as a great ally in the search for theological method. Other churchmen have pointed to the limitations of science, and to its frequent utilisation, not in the service of mankind but in widening the differences between developed and developing countries. The ambiguity of scientific research is exemplified most dramatically in nuclear technology. To despair of man's creativity would be to despair of his creator, to bury one's head in the sand and to decline. As a gift of God, used in the service of God through the Holy Spirit, science may be a development of inestimable value to mankind. The Church in society may learn from science in theoretical as well as in practical spheres, developing her understanding of the universe, and of man's role in it, in still unimaginable ways.

CHURCH AND CULTURE

On the whole area of Church and society, and Church and culture in the modern world, few theologians have been as profound as the Niebuhr brothers. Reinhold Niebuhr understood as few Christians of his time the complex pressures at work in a society of vast corporations, different ethnic groups, shifting, conflicting and often highly irrational political pressures.[4] Against such a background of deterministic pressures the individual, however sincere and upright in his personal life, is all too easily manipulated and pressured into the moral twilight of the world of great institutions. Yet great institutions are necessary for the welfare of modern society. How is the Church to act? Niebuhr saw clearly the corporate nature of sin, and the fatal ability of simple and upright Christians to engage corporately in exploiting their fellows in the business, commercial and social spheres. Against this he recalled men to the grace of the transcendent God of Jesus Christ, understood not simply as a support for family devotion but as a focus for developing the whole life of a great industrial nation.

In some ways even more subtle is the reflection on the role of the Church in society which runs through the work of his brother, H. R. Niebuhr. Richard Niebuhr understood the whole of modern culture, its art, literature, politics, social life, as a field in which creation should be shot through with new creation, in which fulfilment through Christ should bring a new cultural richness. In all his work, and notably in different ways in *Christ and Culture* and *The Kingdom of God in America*, he stressed the integral role of the Church of Jesus Christ in the development of the political, ethical and social structures of a nation. The Church has a prophetic role in society. It is called to promote the increase among men of the love of God and neighbour. If it fails here, it will be the first to suffer divine condemnation.[5]

14 The household of faith and the knowledge of God

EXPERIENCE OF GOD AND MAN

No man or woman can believe for another. Faith is a personal gift and a personal responsibility, given in the mystery of personal relationship with a personal God. Yet faith which is solitary and individual is always at risk of excessive introspection and egoism. In exceptional circumstances, this solitary faith is a gift of limitless value. But the more normal fulfilment of Christian faith is faith together with others, in community. True humanity is co-humanity. The experience of life, worship and service together with others leads to a deepening of faith's knowledge of God.

The Church, then, is not only a vehicle of Christian worship and service, but it may be itself a means of grace, a help to us in deepening understanding. Faith is a completely human insight as well as a gift of God's spirit. The Holy Spirit operates in, with and under human nature in strengthening faith. Of course, without the faith of others in the past the Christian faith would not have come down to us as it has. God has used past generations as the instruments of his message of salvation, and he speaks again to each generation through human contact. Experience, and shared experience, is an important source and ground of Christian belief. Such shared experience does not amount to knowledge, of the sort for which Christians hope after death. But the sharing of experience leads to a deepening of reflection and a maturity of understanding, which is part of the concrete realisation of the communion of saints.

There are many varieties of religious experience. All of these, like all things human, are subject to self-deception and misrepresentation. But they may become instruments of the knowledge of God in a variety of ways. Often religious experience is inarticulate and is shared without explicit discussion. Living life with a tacit common purpose of trying, however inadequately, to become a channel of God's love in the life of family and community, countless people have come to reflect with gratitude on a deepening sense of the hidden presence of God in human life. The problem of evil in numerous forms raises sharp questions, and drives to further reflection. But the shared experience of faith may bring a sense of purpose, determination and peace in the most trying of circumstances. This is not always the case. We do no service to God's love for men by forgetting the clouds of depression and blank despair which overwhelm many people for so much of the time. However shabby its credentials in terms of its own efforts, the household of faith in Christian community remains a basic means of helping people towards a deeper knowledge of God, and this is its most central function.

Christians have long reflected on the hidden love of God. God is a hidden God whose presence is a mysterious and unique presence, simultaneously personal and transcendent. Our language about God is built up largely by analogy with objects in our world of imagination and perception. It is not merely symbolic, because of the reality of God's presence in the history of Israel and through his unique engagement with humanity in the life, death and resurrection of Jesus Christ. But symbols play a necessary role in reflecting the variety of responses within the household of faith to the knowledge of God in Christ.

Symbols of transcendence are related to the cultures which produce them and come and go with these cultures. At various times different symbols serve to preserve the centre of faith against inadequate interpretation. None is entirely adequate. Symbols are not barriers to critical reflection but a stimulus to deepened reflection on and loyalty to God. There has been much controversy recently in Britain about the value of christological symbols, in debates about incarnation, myth and God. The major objections to theories supporting or rejecting the symbols often involve an inadequate grasp of what Christians have been trying to express. Here sincerity, on either side, is no substitute for some appreciation of the profoundly mysterious nature of God's love. God is not 'just like' any simple, convenient example of objects of empirical knowledge.

PRAYER AND DISCIPLESHIP

The most basic feature of the relationship between the Church as the household of God and the Christian knowledge of God is to be observed not in the sphere of argument but in the sphere of prayer. Prayer is talking to God, and communication is of the essence of personal relationship. It is no accident that some of the most illuminating discussion of God in history takes place in the context of prayer. One thinks of Augustine's *Confessions*: 'What man will teach men to understand? We must ask it of thee. Only thus shall we find truth, only thus shall the door be opened.'[1] The same tone is the hallmark of St Anselm's *Proslogion*, and one could add many other instances.

> Teach me to seek thee, and when I seek thee show thyself to me, for I cannot seek thee unless thou teach me, or find thee unless thou show me thyself. Let me seek thee in my desire, let me desire thee in my seeking. Let me find thee by loving thee, let me love thee when I find thee.[2]

In the first volume of his recent *Systematic Theology*, Gerhard Ebeling has a long and fascinating section on the hidden presence of God.[3] He sees prayer as the key to the doctrine of God, corresponding in its hidden spiritual nature to the hiddenness of divine grace. He stresses the connection between faith, prayer, the knowledge of God and the service of men.

> Lord, increase my faith as a grain of mustard seed. Let it not be dead, nor temporary, nor feigned; but a faith that worketh through love, an by deeds, that ministers to virtue, and conquers the world, a faith most holy.[4]

There is a world of difference, indeed several possible worlds, between the work of Ebeling, pupil of Bonhoeffer and theologian concerned for the interpretation of Christian faith in a secular world, and the work of the seventeenth century bishop Lancelot Andrewes quoted above. To make any connection between these worlds is to invite the risk of pietism or romanticism. My intention is not, however, an invitation to the delights of Barchester but a suggestion of the continued absolute centrality of the Christian tradition of trust in God's grace, even in the bleakest frontiers of our modern secular world. The mission of the Church as I understand it, called into and out of the world, requires the concentration of all the various strands of its spiritual heritage, its traditions working in concerned rather than contradictory directions, if it is not to be the classical example of the unprofitable servant. Ours is a time for concentration and deliberate effort rather than timidity and dilettantism. Judgement doubtless still begins in the house of the Lord.

Prayer, then, is not the end of a conversation about the Church but a beginning. Through prayer we can see again the need for a critical faith, and for a critical appraisal by the Church of its role in understanding God and serving as the instrument of his love. Through prayer we may begin to see that though with men, scholars, churchmen, theologians, books, nothing can be done, with God things are not only possible but in fact take place.

This perspective of knowledge within the household of prayer and faith, despite appearances, was well summed up by Rudolf Bultmann, radical scholar and member of the Confessing Church.

> In the face of this great contradiction, faith persistently affirms its great 'Nevertheless' which can honestly be declared by anyone who has decisively encountered the love of God in Christ, the love which has redeemed him from the bondage of himself. In this situation he will surrender his thought to God, not by renouncing his reasoning powers in all those areas of life which reason can investigate and know, but by renouncing the attempt to shape his course in life by reason alone, by surrendering the presumption to solve life's mysteries.[5]

Not least, then, among the functions of the Church of the love of God is the deepening of the knowledge of God. In the life and fate of Jesus of Nazareth in the past we see the character of God's love. God's identification with mankind through the history of Israel reaches a climax in Jesus' death, where love is made available to all men and women, regardless of their own reaction to God. In human life in community, self-giving may involve self-sacrifice to the point of destruction. So it does for God, but in the Resurrection God's purpose for humanity, reflecting his own nature, is seen to be worked out in self-fulfilment, self-giving producing freedom.

It might well be argued that no amount of experience of love, present or future, can make up for all the evils which have befallen the human community since then, and which God has not prevented. The Christian Church as the household of God, after Auschwitz and whatever comes next, can only point with renewed urgency to the suffering love of God on the cross, and attempt to spell out the meaning of discipleship, of the Church of the love of God today, in a corresponding manner of commitment.

That is why continuing to work away at doctrines of the Church in theory and above all in practice, can never be a waste of time, despite often almost all appearances to the contrary. We need not abandon too lightly to the fashions of the day the faith that God has been involved in the work of his Church, and will go on with those in the future who seek to be led in the way of discipleship.

Notes

(See too the bibliographies for each chapter)

CHAPTER I (pp. 1–8)

1 Segundo, in *The Church Called Community*, New York, 1973, p. 3, makes the point that the Church has existed only for a tiny fraction of the time in which man has been on this planet.

2 On biblical fundamentalism cf. James Barr, *Fundamentalism*, London, 1977. The arguments may be applied equally to other sorts of fundamentalism.

3 See my *Theology of the Love of God*, London, 1980.

4 See Bonhoeffer, *Letters and Papers from Prison*, and *Ethics*.

5 Karl Barth, *For the Freedom of the Gospel*, TEH2, 1933, 6.

6 Cf. James T. Burtchaell, *Catholic Theories of Biblical Inspiration since 1810*, Cambridge, 1969.

CHAPTER 2 (pp. 9–14)

1 B. Wasserstein, *Britain and the Jews of Europe*, Oxford, 1979.

2 See Kurt Nowak, *Euthanasia and Sterilisation in the Third Reich*, Göttingen, 1978.

3 Vonnegut, op. cit., p. 32f.

4 See Don Cupitt, *Crisis of Moral Authority*, London, 1972, 48f.

5 G. W. H. Lampe, *God as Spirit*, Oxford, 1977, 203.

6 K. Rahner, *Theological Investigations 16*, London, 1979.

7 Karl Barth, *Kirchliche Dogmatik*. IV/4.31.

CHAPTER 3 (pp. 15–24)

1 See Ernest Best, *The Body*, London, 1955.

2 See Paul S. Minear, *Images of the Church*, London, 1961.

3 See G. Bornkamm, *Jesus of Nazareth*, London, 1960.

4 The literature is enormous. See especially H. E. Todt, *The Son of Man in the Synoptic Gospels*, London, 1965.

5 R. Bultmann, *St John's Gospel*, London, 1971.

6 See the commentaries by C. L. Mitton, H. Chadwick, H. Schlier, etc.

CHAPTER 4 (pp. 25–32)

1 See Hans von Campenhausen's masterly study, *Ecclesiastical Authority and Spiritual Power*, London, 1969.
2 See Walter Bauer, *Orthodoxy and Heresy in Earliest Christianity*, London, 1973.
3 The theology of the Donatists is summarised in the Rules of Tyconius, ed. F. C. Burkitt, Cambridge, 1894.
4 See his great work *The City of God*, London, Everyman, 1945.
5 See especially *The Babylonian Captivity of the Church*, and *The Heidelberg Disputation*.
6 See R. S. Wallace, *Calvin*, Marshall, Morgan and Scott, London (forthcoming).
7 The Barmen Declaration. Cf. W. Niesel, *Reformed Symbolics*, Edinburgh, 1962, p. 357f.

CHAPTER 5 (pp. 33–41)

1 See especially E. Busch, *Karl Barth*, London, 1976.
2 There is much unpublished research on Küng, e.g. *The Church in the Thought of H. Küng*, G. A. Turner, Princeton, *STM* 1967. For literature on Moltmann, Küng and Ramsey see bibliographies.
3 Rahner in *Diskussion über Christ Sein*, see also *Diskussion über Die Kirche*.
4 Ramsey, *Canterbury Pilgrim*, London, 1974, p. 107.
5 Ramsey, *The Future of the Christian Church*, p. 23.

CHAPTER 6 (pp. 42–47)

1 See H. von Campenhausen, *Ecclesiastical Authority and Spiritual Power*, London, 1969.
2 J. Moltmann, *The Church in the Power of the Spirit*, London.
3 H. Küng, *The Church*, London.
4 A. M. Ramsey, *Holy Spirit*, London, 1977, p. 87.

CHAPTER 7 (pp. 48–55)

1 See R. Niebuhr, *Schleiermacher on Christ and Religion*, London 1965, and S. W. Sykes, *Friedrich Schleiermacher*, London, 1971.
2 Ramsey, *The Gospel and the Catholic Church*, pp. 98ff. and *The Great Christian Centuries*.
3 Küng, *The Church*, p. 219.
4 Moltmann, *The Church in the Power of the Spirit*, p. 258.
5 London, 1951.
6 N. L. A. Lash, *His Presence in the World*, London, 1968, pp. 117, 148.

CHAPTER 8 (pp. 56–62)

1 Ed. G. D. Henderson, Edinburgh, 1960.
2 London, 1967.
3 *The Church Inside Out*, London, 1967, p. 27.

CHAPTER 9 (pp. 63–76)

1 *Systematic Theology* III, London, 1957, p. 400f.
2 *The Social Sources of Denominationalism.*
3 *Power without Glory*, London, 1967.
4 The Hague, 1977.
5 See H. J. Marx, *Filioque und Verbot eines anderen Glaubens*, on the council of Florence, Cologne, 1977.
6 Henderson, op. cit., p. 104.
7 London, 1979.
8 London, 1978.
9 *Church Sacraments and Ministry*, London, 1975, p. 98.
10 I am grateful to my wife for the use of a paper on this topic.
11 Dr. G. Leonard, Speech for General Synod of the Church of England (*Church Times*, Nov. 10th 1978).
12 *The Month*, February 1977.

CHAPTER 10 (pp. 77–81)

1 E. Schillebeeckx, *Christ the Sacrament*, London, 1975.
2 *Church Dogmatics*, IV/2.55 and IV/1.58.
3 *De Doctrina Christiana*. 2.3.4.

CHAPTER 11 (pp. 82–91)

1 See my *Hilary of Poitiers*, Frankfurt, 1978, pp. 160ff.
2 See Barth, *Church Dogmatics*, II/IC Edinburgh.

CHAPTER 12 (pp. 92–97)

1 See my *Theology of the Love of God*, 27f.
2 See in this series *The Christian Hope*, by B. L. Hebblethwaite, forthcoming.

CHAPTER 13 (pp. 98–104)

1 For Hegel see especially T. Rendtorff, *Church and Theology*, London, 1970.
2 See E. R. Norman, *Christianity and the World Order*, London, 1978.
3 See for example *Christianity in World Perspective*, London, 1968.
4 R. Niebuhr, *The Nature and Destiny of Man, Moral Man in Immoral Society, An Interpretation of Christian Ethics, The Children of Light and the Children of Darkness.* On Reinhold Niebuhr see B. L. Hebblethwaite, *The Adequacy of Christian Ethics*, London, 1981.
5 H. R. Niebuhr, see bibliography.

CHAPTER 14 (pp. 105–109)

1 St Augustine, *Confessions*, end. (Bk. 13.38).
2 St Anselm, *Proslogion*, chapter 1.
3 Ebeling, *Die Christliche Dogmatik*, I Tübingen, 1979, pp. 224f.
4 *Lancelot Andrewes and his Private Devotions*, ed. Alexander Whyte, London, 1896, p. 168.
5 Bultmann, *This World and Beyond* (Marburg Sermons), London, 1960, pp. 165–6.

Select Bibliography

It is hoped that this section may help the reader to pursue further in depth some of the central themes discussed in the preceding text.

1 What is the Christian Church?
Apart from the studies mentioned in Chapter 5, one might mention, from thousands of books, L. S. Thornton, *The Common Life in the Body of Christ*, London, 1942; R. N. Flew, *The Nature of the Church*, London, 1952; L. Newbigin, *The Household of God*, London, 1957; C. Welch, *The Reality of the Church*, 1958; T. F. Torrance, *Conflict and Agreement in the Church*, 2 vols., London, 1959; K. Rahner, *The Shape of the Church to Come*, London, 1974; A. Dulles, *Models of the Church*, Dublin, 1977; E. Schlink, *The Coming Christ and the Coming Church*, Edinburgh, 1967; A. T. Hanson, *Church, Sacraments and Ministry*, London, 1975. There are sections in all the systematic theologies, e.g. in the work of Barth, Tillich, Rahner, Weber, Schmaus, Segundo.

2 The Church as the death of the gospel?
Some of the most telling critique is in great literature, e.g. in Ibsen and Dostoevsky. See too such studies as Bryan Wilson, *Religion in Secular Society*, 1966, and M. Machovec, *A Marxist Looks at Jesus*, London, 1976. For a Christian response see J. C. Hoekendijk, *The Church Inside Out*, London, 1967; *Toward Vatican III*, by Küng, Tracy and Metz, Dublin, 1978; D. Jenkins, *The Contradiction of Christianity*, London, 1976; D. Bonhoeffer, *Sanctorum Communio*, London, 1963. On the Holy Spirit see, apart from the systematic theologies, G. S. Hendry, *The Holy Spirit in Christian Theology*, 1965; G. W. H. Lampe, *God as Spirit*, 1977; A. M. Ramsey, *The Holy Spirit*, 1977; K. Rahner, *The Spirit in the Church*, 1974.

3 The Church: the biblical foundation
On the material in general see P. S. Minear, *Images of the Church in the New Testament*, London, 1960 and K. L. Schmidt, *Ecclesia*, London, 1950. On Jesus in the New Testament, G. Bornkamm, *Jesus of Nazareth*, London, 1960, is still the standard work. Issues of church order, Jesus and the Church, and the theology of the Church are inevitably interrelated, regardless of the professed objectivity of the study. A varied selection might include such works as F. J. Hort, *The Christian Ecclesia*, 1897; R. Schnackenburg, *The Church in the New Testament*, 1974; G. Johnston, *The Doctrine of the Church in the New Testament*, 1943; E. Käsemann, *The Testament of Jesus*, 1976; E.

Schweizer, *Church Order in the New Testament*, 1961; E. Best, *One Body in Christ*, 1955; E. Mersch, *The Theology of the Mystical Body*, 1952; D. Cupitt, *Jesus and the Gospel of God*, 1979.

4 *The test of history*
Apart from the histories of doctrine, like Lietzmann, or Chadwick (Pelican), such works as L. Goppelt, *Apostolic and Post-Apostolic Times*, 1970; S. L. Greenslade, *Schism in the Early Church*, 1953; W. Bauer, *Orthodoxy and Heresy in the Early Church*, 1973; V. Lossky, *The Mystical Theology of the Eastern Church*, 1967; Peter Brown, *Augustine*, 1967; M. D. Chenu, *Towards Understanding St Thomas*, 1950; H. Obermann, *Forerunners of the Reformation*, 1976; G. Ebeling, *Luther*, 1970; F. Wendel, *Calvin*, 1963; G. H. Williams, *The Radical Reformation*, 1962; F. Heyer, *The Catholic Church 1648–1870*, 1968; B. C. Butler, *The Vatican Council 1869–70*, 1962; O. Chadwick, *The Victorian Church*, 1966–70; T. Rendtorff, *Church and Theology*, 1970; E. Bethge, *Dietrich Bonhoeffer*, 1970; G. Rupp, *Protestant Catholicity*, 1960; J. Pelikan, *Obedient Rebels*, 1963.

5 *The Church Now: Moltmann, Küng and Ramsey*
See J. Moltmann, *The Church in the Power of the Spirit, The Crucified God, Theology of Hope*; Küng, *The Church, Structures of the Church, Why Priests?, On Being a Christian, Infallibility, Truthfulness, Justification*; A. M. Ramsey, *The Gospel and the Catholic Church* London, 1974, *Canterbury Pilgrim*, London, 1974, *The Future of the Church, Great Christian Centuries to Come*, London, 1974, *The Holy Spirit*, London, 1977. There are discussion volumes in German on the major works of Moltmann and Küng.

6 *The Christian ministry*
Again the selection is enormous. A few are H. von Campenhausen, *Ecclesiastical Authority and Spiritual Power*, London, 1969; T. M. Lindsay, *Church and Ministry in the Early Centuries*, 1902; O. Cullmann, *Peter*, 1968; O. Karrer, *Peter and the Church*, 1968; R. C. Moberly, *Ministerial Priesthood*, 1897; T. W. Manson, *Ministry and Priesthood*, 1958; G. Dix, *The Shape of the Liturgy*, 1958; ed. K. E. Kirk, *The Apostolic Ministry*, 1946.

7 *Christ, word and sacrament*
A. J. B. Higgins, *The Lord's Supper in the New Testament*, 1952; K. Rahner, *The Church and the Sacraments*, in *Studies in Modern Theology*, 1964; N. Lash, *His Presence in the World*, 1967; D. M. Baillie, *Theology of the Sacraments*, 1952?; E. L. Mascall, *Corpus Christi*, 1963; J. MacQuarrie, *An Existentialist Theology*, 1955, pp. 224f. Also K. Barth, *Church Dogmatics* IV/4, etc.; J. K. Mozley, *The Gospel Sacraments*, 1933; R. Bruce, *Sermons on the Lord's Supper*, ed. T. F. Torrance, 1958; G. Ebeling, *The Word of God and Tradition*, 1964; J. McLeod Campbell, *Christ the Bread of Life*, 1959; Bernard Leeming, *Principles of Sacramental Theology*, 1956.

8 *Structuring elements of doctrine: the Church*
See the World Council of Churches' Faith and Order literature of the Church, especially Louvain 1971. G. O'Grady, *The Church in the Theology of Karl Barth, The Church in Roman Catholic Theology*, 2 vols., 1968–70; *The Doctrine of the Church*, ed. D. G. Kilpatrick, London, 1964. On ecumenical theology see ed. D. M. Baillie and J. Marsh, *Intercommunion*, London, 1952; Ed. R. Rouse and S. C. Neill, *A History of the Ecumenical Movement*, 1954. On dangers in ecumenism see I. Henderson, *Power Without Glory*, London, 1961. See also G. A. Lindbeck, *The Future of Roman Catholic Theology*, 1969; S. W. Sykes, *The Integrity of Anglicanism*, 1978; M. Fouyas, *Orthodoxy, Roman Catholicism and Anglicanism*, 1972; K. T. Ware, *The Orthodox Church*, 1963. See too the reports of the various ecumenical negotiations and unions, G. D. Henderson, *The Claims of the Church of Scotland*, A. Clark and C. Davey, *Anglican/Roman Catholic Dialogue*, 1974. On the problem of authority see Campenhausen, ed. R. R. Williams, *Authority in the Church* (especially the essay by I. T. Ramsey); N. Lash, *Voices of Authority*, 1976; and the essays on Authority in *Ecumenical Review* 1969.

9 *Structuring elements of doctrine: ministry*
See under section 6. Useful but untranslated is G. Gassmann, *Das historischeBishofsamt und die Einheit der Kirche*, Göttingen, 1964. On the ordination of women see K. Bliss, *The Service and Status of Women in the Churches*, 1952; *Women Priests Now*, 1978; and the various reports of church bodies. On Ministry see too K. Rahner, *Bishops*, 1963; T. W. Manson, *The Church's Ministry*, 1948.

10 *Structuring elements of doctrine: sacraments*
See above. See too for Roman Catholic theology E. Yarnold, *The Second Gift, a Study of Grace*, London, 1974. On Baptism: G. W. H. Lambe, *The Seal of the Spirit*, 1951.

11 *The Church in Christian community*
See sections 1, 2 and 5. Also such works as G. Wingren, *Gospel and Church*; F. Olofsson, *Christus Redemptor et Consummator*, a study in the theology of B. F. Westcott, Uppsala 1979; biographies of, for example, John White, Phillips Brooks, William Temple, etc. See F. W. Dillistone, *The Christian Understanding of Atonement*, 1968; S. Kierkegaard, *Training in Christianity*, D. M. Baillie, *Faith in God*, 1927. A. van den Heuvel, *The Humiliation of the Church*, 1966; D. Bonhoeffer, *The Cost of Discipleship*.

13 *The Church in society*
See such works as R. Robertson, *The Sociological Interpretation of Religion*, Oxford, 1972; T. Eagleton, *The New Left Church*, 1966; E. R. Norman, *Christianity and the World Order*, 1978; H. Cox, *The Secular City*, 1966; F. Gray, *Divine Disobedience*, 1970; H. R. Niebuhr, *Christ and Culture*, etc.; Reinhold Niebuhr, *The Nature and Destiny of Man*, etc.

14 *The household of faith and the knowledge of God*
See Ebeling, *Die Christliche Dogmatik*, I, etc.; K. Barth, *Prayer and Preaching*, London, 1964.

Articles in dictionaries are often helpful in enabling one to grasp quickly the scope of the issues. In this connection older works, such as Hastings' *Encyclopedia of Religion and Ethics* should not be despised. I have limited the list to material in English or in English translation.
Other works of interest in the field might include the following:
The Universal Church in God's Design, London, 1948, (WCC).
D. T. Jenkins, *The Gift of the Ministry*, London, 1947.
A. T. Hanson, *The Pioneer Ministry*, London, 1961.
K. E. Skydsgaard, *One in Christ*, 1957.
E. Hatch, *The Organisation of the Early Christian Church*, 1880.
B. H. Streeter, *The Primitive Church*, 1929.
A. C. Quick, *The Christian Sacraments*, 1927.
R. S. Louden, *The True Face of the Kirk*, 1963.
W. Pannenberg, *The Kingdom of God*, 1977.
K. Rahner, 'Theology of Symbol', in *Theological Investigations 4. Theological Investigations 16*, on the Holy Spirit.
Ed. H. R. Niebuhr and D. D. Williams, *The Ministry in Historical Perspective*, New York, 1956.
F. J. Taylor, *The Church of God*, 1946.
Vatican II. Documents. Ed. W. M. Abbott, London/New York, 1966.
M. Wiles, 'Eucharistic Theology – The Value of Diversity', in *Explorations in Theology 4*, London, 1979.
E. Troeltsch, *The Social Teaching of the Christian Churches*, 1912.
M. A. Thung, *Precarious Organisation*, The Hague, 1974.
P. Lehmann, *Ethics in a Christian Context*, 1963.
On H. R. Niebuhr, *Faith and Ethics*, ed. P. Ramsey, New York, 1957.
J. W. Fowler, *To See the Kingdom*, 1976.
L. Hoedemaker, *The Theology of H. R. Niebuhr*, 1970.
T. H. Sanks, *Authority in the Church*, AAR/Scholars Press, 1974.
T. B. Ommen, *The Hermeneutics of Dogma*, AAR/Scholars Press, 1975.
H. Gollwitzer, *Coena Domini*, 1940, untranslated but excellent on Luther and Calvin.
J. H. Newman, *Tract 90* and *The Development of Christian Doctrine*.
N. L. A. Lash, *Doctrine in Focus*: a study in the development of doctrine, London, 1973.
Claude Welch, *Protestant Thought in the Nineteenth Century*, 1973.
J. Pelikan, *The Riddle of Roman Catholicism*, 1960.
S. Neill, *Twentieth Century Christianity*, 1962.
J. Kent and R. Murray, eds. *Church Membership and Intercommunion*, 1973.
A. Harnack, *Thoughts on Protestantism*, 1899.
W. Nicholls, *Ecumenism and Catholicity*, 1952.
J. P. Mackey, *The Modern Theology of Tradition*, London, 1962.
P. Berger, *A Rumour of Angels*, 1969.
J. Baillie, *Baptism and Conversion*, 1964.

Select Bibliography

G. H. Tavard, *Two Centuries of Ecumenism*, Notre Dame, 1962.
J. Jeremias, *Infant Baptism in the First Four Centuries*, 1960.
A. R. Vidler, *The Church in an Age of Revolution*, 1961.
T. F. Torrance, *Kingdom and Church*, Edinburgh, 1965.
E. Wolf, *Peregrinatio I, II*, untranslated. Excellent on Lutheran tradition, Munich 1954, 1965.
T. F. Torrance, *Theology in Reconciliation*, London, 1976.
C. E. Raven, *The Gospel and the Church*, London, 1940.
H. G. C. Moule, *Nicholas Ridley on the Lord's Supper*, London, 1895.
G. H. Tavard, *Holy Writ or Holy Church*, London, 1959.
Ed. K. Ware and C. Davey, *Anglican-Orthodox Dialogue*, London, 1977.
Ed. R. S. Anderson, *Theological Foundations for Ministry*, Edinburgh/Grand Rapids 1979.
H. V. Richardson, *Dark Salvation*, New York, 1976.
W. Pannenberg, *Ethik und Ekklesiologie*, Göttingen, 1977.
P. Chirico, *Infallibility*, London, 1976.
C. Ernst, *The Multiple Echo*, London, 1979.

Index